**The Johns Hopkins Comparative Nonprofit Sector Project**

# Global Civil Society
## An Overview

Lester M. Salamon
S. Wojciech Sokolowski
Regina List

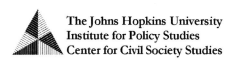

The Johns Hopkins University
Institute for Policy Studies
Center for Civil Society Studies

ISBN 1-886333-50-5

Center for Civil Society Studies
Institute for Policy Studies
The Johns Hopkins University
3400 N. Charles Street
Baltimore, MD 21218-2688, USA

# Preface

This report summarizes the basic empirical results of the latest phase of the Johns Hopkins Comparative Nonprofit Sector Project, the major effort we have had under way for a number of years to document the scope, structure, financing, and role of the nonprofit sector for the first time in various parts of the world, and to explain the resulting patterns that exist.

This phase of project work has focused primarily on 15 countries in Africa, the Middle East, and South Asia, 13 of which are covered here. In addition to reporting on these 13 countries, however, this report puts these findings into the broader context of our prior work. It therefore provides a portrait of the "civil society sector" in 35 countries throughout the world, including 16 advanced industrial countries, 14 developing countries, and 5 transitional countries of Central and Eastern Europe.

While important, the descriptive empirical results reported here do not exhaust the focus of the work we have under way. Rather, this work has also pursued two additional goals: first, to determine the causes of the diverse patterns of civil society sector development described here; and second, to assess the impact of the civil society sector. Subsequent products of this project will explore the findings on these latter two objectives. Even the present report is designed to be the overview chapter in a longer publication, moreover. This longer publication, the second volume of our earlier book, Global Civil Society: Dimensions of the Nonprofit Sector, will include chapters exploring in greater depth the contours of the civil society sector in each of the individual countries covered in this latest phase of our project.[1] We have chosen to make this overview of the basic descriptive results of this phase of our work available immediately in view of the considerable interest that has been shown in them throughout the world.

As the body of this brief report makes clear, we use the terms "civil society sector" or "civil society organization" to refer to a broad array of organizations that are essentially private, i.e., outside the institutional structures of government; that are not primarily commercial and do not exist primarily to distribute profits to their directors or "owners"; that are self-governing; and that people are free to join or support voluntarily. This definition was formulated in collaboration with teams of researchers and advisors from around the world and has been used successfully to guide field work in over 40 countries. Informal as well as formally registered organizations are included within this definition as is the informal input of volunteers as well as the more formal effort of paid staff. Similarly, the definition embraces religious as well as secular organizations.

I am grateful to the extraordinary team of colleagues involved in the Johns Hopkins Comparative Nonprofit Sector Project for their invaluable assistance in generating the information reported here. Special thanks are owed to the Local Associates listed in Appendix C for assisting us in formulating the basic project concepts, in adapting them to the diverse realities of their countries, in generating the needed data, and in interpreting what they found.

Thanks are also due to my colleagues in the Johns Hopkins Center for Civil Society Studies who contributed significantly to this product. These include my co-authors, Wojciech Sokolowski and Regina List, but also Stefan Toepler, who coordinated the data gathering in the Middle Eastern countries; Leslie Hems, who coordinated the data gathering in Pakistan; and Mimi Bilzor and Claudine DiPeppe, who coordinated and assisted with, respectively, the production of this document.

Finally, I gratefully acknowledge the financial support provided by the organizations listed in Appendix E and the advice and counsel provided by the numerous experts on the nonprofit sector and philanthropy who have served on the national and international advisory committees to this project.

None of these people or organizations, nor any others with which I am affiliated, bears responsibility for any errors of fact or interpretation that this document might contain, however. That responsibility is mine alone.

Lester M. Salamon
Annapolis, Maryland
March 16, 2003

---

[1] For publication details on this broader volume, visit our Web site: www.jhu.edu/~ccss.

# Global Civil Society: An Overview

Lester M. Salamon, S. Wojciech Sokolowski, and Regina List

## INTRODUCTION

Recent years have witnessed a considerable surge of interest throughout the world in the broad range of institutions that occupy the social space between the market and the state. Known variously as the "nonprofit," the "voluntary," the "civil society," the "third," the "social economy," the "NGO," or the "charitable" sector, this set of institutions includes within it a sometimes bewildering array of entities—hospitals, universities, social clubs, professional organizations, day care centers, grassroots development organizations, health clinics, environmental groups, family counseling agencies, self-help groups, religious congregations, sports clubs, job training centers, human rights organizations, community associations, soup kitchens, homeless shelters, and many more.

Despite their diversity, these entities share important common features that justify thinking of them as a distinctive set of institutions, as an identifiable social "sector." For one thing, they are private in character and not part of the governmental apparatus. But unlike other private institutions, these entities are expected to serve some public or community purpose and not simply to generate profits for those involved in them. They therefore embody two seemingly contradictory impulses: first, a commitment to freedom and personal initiative, to the idea that people have the right to act on their own authority to improve the quality of their own lives or the lives of persons they care about; and second, an emphasis on solidarity, on the idea that people have responsibilities not only to themselves but also to the communities of which they are a part. Uniquely among social institutions, the institutions of the nonprofit or civil society sector merge these two impulses, producing a set of private institutions serving essentially public purposes.

## The "global associational revolution"

The existence of such institutions is by no means a new phenomenon. Nonprofit or charitable institutions have long operated in societies throughout the world, the product of religious impulses, social movements, cultural or professional interests, sentiments of solidarity and mutuality, altruism, and, more recently, government's need for assistance to carry out public functions. Yet the number and variety of such organizations seem to have grown enormously in recent years. Indeed, a veritable "global associational revolution" appears to be under way, a massive upsurge of organized private, voluntary activity in virtually every region of the world—in the developed countries of North America, Western Europe, and Asia; throughout Central and Eastern Europe; and in much of the developing world.[2] The rise of the civil society sector may, in fact, prove to be as significant a development of the late twentieth and early twenty-first centuries as the rise of the nation-state was of the late nineteenth and early twentieth centuries.

What lies behind this development is a wide assortment of different factors. For one thing, recent dramatic breakthroughs in information technology and literacy have awakened people to the realization that their circumstances may not be immutable, that opportunities may be better elsewhere, and that change is possible. They have also made it easier to form the organizations through which to translate these sentiments into effective social action. This has stimulated citizen activism; awakened gender, environmental, and ethnic consciousness; and prompted heightened interest in human rights.

At the same time, dissatisfaction has grown with both the market and the state as mechanisms to solve the interrelated social, economic, and environmental crises of our time. The state stands accused of stifling initiative, creating unresponsive bureaucracies, and generally absorbing escalating shares of national income. The market, on the other hand, has been criticized for ignoring human need and producing untenable social inequalities. The result has been an increasingly frantic search for a "middle way" between sole reliance on the market and sole reliance on the state to cope with public problems—a search that is evident in Prime Minister Tony Blair's emphasis on a "Third Way" in the U.K., Gerhard Schröder's "New Middle" in Germany, and strategies emphasizing empowerment of the poor and "assisted self-reliance" in the developing world. French Prime Minister Lionel Jospin's summary declaration: "Yes to a market economy, no to a market society" seems to summarize the prevailing sentiment well.

Because of their unique combination of private structure and public purpose, their generally smaller scale, their connections to citizens, their flexibility, and their capacity to tap private initiative in support of public purposes, civil society organizations have surfaced as strategically important potential partners in the effort to fashion such new solutions, and therefore are "a basic part," as one close observer has put it, "of the politics of the third way."[3]

Also contributing to the attention such organizations have attracted is recent research suggesting that these organizations contribute importantly to the production of "social capital," those bonds of trust and reciprocity that have been found to be critical preconditions for democracy and economic growth.[4] Fears about a decline, or general insufficiency, of such trust have come to be a major preoccupation in countries throughout the world, leading to increased interest in not-for-profit organizations as a way to help remedy the deficit.

The growth of civil society organizations has also been significantly enhanced by the expansion of the pool of educated professionals in many parts of the world in the 1960s and 1970s. Faced with repressive political regimes and limited economic opportunities, especially after the oil shock of the early 1970s, many of these individuals came to see in nongovernmental organizations a vehicle through which to make a difference in their societies. In doing so, they helped convert the demand for civil society organizations into an actual supply of them.

Finally, a variety of external actors have helped to move the process along, often providing crucial financial and human resources to support the resulting civil society activity. Included here have been liberal elements in the Catholic Church, which played an important role in stimulating the formation of grassroots community groups throughout Latin America in the aftermath of the Castro Revolution of 1959; Western charitable foundations committed to grassroots democracy and empowerment of the poor; multinational corporations eager to ensure a "license" to operate in far-away lands; and, in more recent years, multilateral organizations like the World Bank that have come to recognize the need to engage citizen energies to implement their development agendas.

## The problem

Despite their growing presence and importance, however, civil society organizations have long been the lost continent on the social landscape of our world. Only recently have they attracted serious attention in policy circles or the press, and even academic interest has surfaced only in recent years. Even now, social and political discourse remains heavily dominated by a "two-sector model" that acknowledges the existence of only two social spheres outside of the family unit—the market and the state, or business and government. This has been reinforced by statistical conventions that have kept this "third sector" of civil society organizations largely invisible in official economic statistics.[5] Even the most basic information about these organizations—their numbers, size, activities, economic weight, finances, and role—has therefore been lacking in most places, while deeper understanding of the factors that contribute to their growth and decline has been almost nonexistent. As a consequence, the civil society sector's ability to participate in the significant policy debates now under way has been seriously hampered and its potential for contributing to the solution of pressing problems too often challenged or ignored.

## The Johns Hopkins Comparative Nonprofit Sector Project

To help fill the resulting gap in basic knowledge about the scope and structure of the third sector internationally, we launched an ambitious international project—the Johns Hopkins Comparative Nonprofit Sector Project—in 1991. Initially focused on thirteen countries—eight developed and five developing—this project has since been extended to over forty countries.

## Objectives

From the outset, this project has sought to accomplish five principal objectives:

- First, to *document* the scope, structure, financing, and role of the civil society sector for the first time in solid empirical terms in a significant number of countries representing different geographic regions, cultural and historical traditions, and of development;
- Second, to *explain* why this sector varies in size, composition, character, and role from place to place and identify the factors that seem to encourage or retard its development, including differences in history, legal arrangements, religious background, cultures, socio-economic structures, and patterns of government policy;
- Third, to *evaluate* the impact these organizations are having and the contributions they make, as well as the drawbacks they entail;
- Fourth, to *improve awareness* of this set of institutions by disseminating the results of the work; and
- Fifth, to *build local capacity* to carry on the work in the future.

## Approach

To pursue these objectives, we formulated an approach that is:

- *Comparative,* covering countries at different levels of development and with a wide assortment of religious, cultural, and political traditions. In particular, work is under way in over 40 countries representing all the continents and most of the world's major religions. Of these, thirty-five have generated results as of this writing. As noted in Table 1, this includes 16 advanced, industrial countries in North America, Western Europe, and Asia; 14 developing countries in Latin America, Africa, the Middle East and South Asia; and five transitional countries of Central and Eastern Europe. This gives the project a wide range of experiences on which to draw in formulating its portrait of the world's third sector and the explanations for its varying patterns of development. More than that, it provides a basis for cross-checking results and for identifying more precisely what makes each country's third sector distinctive. As one analyst has put it: "Thinking without comparison is unthinkable. And, in the absence of comparison, so is all scientific thought and scientific research."[6] Carefully and sensitively done, comparison is thus not simply a technique for understanding others; it is also a necessary step toward understanding oneself.
- *Systematic,* utilizing a common definition of the entities to be included and a common classification system for differentiating among them. Comparison is

**Table 1** Country coverage of the Johns Hopkins Comparative Nonprofit Sector Project

| Developed Countries | | Developing Countries | |
|---|---|---|---|
| Australia | Italy | Argentina | Pakistan |
| Austria | Japan | Brazil | Peru |
| Belgium | Netherlands | Colombia | Philippines |
| Finland | Norway | Egypt | South Africa |
| France | Spain | Kenya | South Korea |
| Germany | Sweden | Mexico | Tanzania |
| Ireland | United States | Morocco | Uganda |
| Israel | United Kingdom | | |

**Transitional Countries**

| | |
|---|---|
| Czech Republic | Romania |
| Hungary | Slovakia |
| Poland | |

only possible if reasonable care is taken in specifying what is to be compared. Given the conceptual ambiguity, lack of knowledge, and ideological overtones that exist in this field, this task naturally had to be approached with care. As outlined more fully below, our approach was to proceed in a bottom-up fashion, building up our definition and classification from the actual experiences of the project countries. The goal throughout was to formulate a definition that is sufficiently broad to encompass the diverse array of entities embraced within this sector in the varied countries we were covering yet sharp enough to differentiate these entities from those that comprise the market and the state, the two other major sectors into which social life has traditionally been divided.

- *Collaborative,* relying extensively on local analysts to root our definitions and analysis in the solid ground of local knowledge and ensure the local experience to carry the work forward in the future. Accordingly, we recruited a principal Local Associate in each country to assist us in all phases of project work (see Appendix C). This included not only data collection and data analysis, but also the formulation of the project's basic conceptual equipment—its working definition, treatment of borderline organizations, classification system, and data-collection strategies. Local Associates met regularly through the life of the project to formulate research strategies, review progress, and fine-tune the approach. These individuals in turn recruited colleagues to assist in the effort. The result was a project team that has engaged at least 150 local researchers around the world in the development and execution of the project's basic tasks.
- *Consultative,* involving the active participation of local civil society activists, government leaders, the press, and the business community in order to further

ensure that the work in each country was responsive to the particular conditions of the country and that the results could be understood and disseminated locally. To achieve this, we organized Advisory Committees in each project country and at the international level (see Appendix D for the membership of the International Advisory Committee). These committees reviewed all aspects of the project approach, assisted in the interpretation of the results, and helped publicize the findings and think through their implications. Altogether, more than 600 nonprofit, philanthropic, government, and business leaders have taken part in the project through these Advisory Committees.

*   *Empirical,* moving wherever possible beyond subjective impressions to develop a body of reasonably solid empirical data on this set of organizations. Obviously, not all facets of the civil society sector can be captured in empirical terms, and some components of the project, such as the legal analysis, the historical analysis, and the "impact" analysis consequently used more qualitative techniques, including case studies, focus groups, and literature review. Nevertheless, given the general confusion that exists in many places about the real scope and structure of this sector, we felt it important to develop as reasonable a set of empirical measures as possible of the overall level of effort that civil society organizations mobilize in each country, the distribution of this effort among various activities, including both service activities and more expressive activities (e.g. policy advocacy, promotion of human rights, arts and culture), and the sources of support for this activity. This required the formulation of a set of research protocols defining the data items being sought and suggesting ways to secure the needed data. It also required the tailoring of these protocols to the realities of the individual countries, a process that was accomplished in collaboration with our Local Associates, as noted more fully below.

**Definition and classification**

Given the comparative and empirical nature of this inquiry, the task of developing a coherent definition of the entities of interest to us took on special importance and therefore deserves special comment. This is particularly true given the somewhat contested nature of the central concepts defining this field. Broadly speaking, three types of definitions of the entities that comprise the "third" or "civil society" sector were available to us, each associated with a particular set of terms.[7] One of these is an essentially *economic definition* that focuses on the *source of organizational support.* According to this definition, a civil society organization is one that receives the predominant portion of its revenue from private contributions, not from market transactions or government support. Terms such as "voluntary sector" or "charitable sector" are sometimes used to convey this sense. A second set of definitions focuses on the *legal status* of the organization. According to this definition, a civil society organization is one that takes a particular legal form (e.g. an "association" or a "foundation") or that is exempted from some or all of a country's taxes. Terms such as "association" or "tax-exempt" organization are often used to convey this sense. Finally, a third set of definitions focuses on the *purposes* such organizations pursue. According to this definition, a civil society organization is one that promotes the public good, encourages empowerment and participation, or seeks to address the structural roots of poverty and distress. Terms such as "civil society" or "NGO" or "charity" are often used to convey this sense.

For a variety of reasons, we found these existing definitions inadequate for the kind of cross-national comparative inquiry we wanted to launch. The economic definitions put too much stress on the revenue sources of civil society organizations, downplaying other features that these organizations share, such as their use of volunteers, their social missions, and their not-for-profit character. The legal definitions, by contrast, are difficult to apply comparatively because each country has its own legal structure, making it difficult to find the comparable classes of entities in the legal frameworks of different countries. And the purpose definitions, while appealing, are too nebulous and subjective to apply in a cross-national analysis, especially since different countries, or different groups of people within countries, have different ideas about what constitutes a valid "public purpose," and it is often difficult to determine whether a particular organization is actually pursuing its avowed purpose anyway. What is more, this kind of definition raises the danger of creating tautologies by making the sector's pursuit of public purposes true *by definition,* rendering it impossible to disprove.

**The structural-operational definition.** In view of these difficulties, we adopted a bottom-up, inductive approach to defining the civil society sector, building up our definition from the actual experiences of the broad range of countries embraced within our project. In particular, we first solicited from our Local Associates a roadmap of the kinds of entities that would reasonably be included in the "third" or "civil society" sector in their respective countries. We then lined these roadmaps up against each other to see where they overlapped and identified the basic characteristics of the entities that fell into this overlapping area. Finally, we made note of the "grey areas" that existed on the fringes of this core concept and created a process for Local Associates to consult with us to determine how to treat entities that occupied these grey areas.

Out of this process emerged a consensus on five structural or operational features that defined the entities at the center of our concern.[8] For the purpose of this project, therefore, we defined the "civil society sector" as composed of entities that are:

- *Organizations*, i.e., they have some structure and regularity to their operations, whether or not they are formally constituted or legally registered. This means that our definition embraces informal, i.e., non-registered, groups as well as formally registered ones. What is important is not whether the group is legally or formally recognized but that it have some organizational permanence and regularity as reflected in regular meetings, a membership, and/or some structure or procedures for taking decisions that participants recognize as legitimate.

- *Private*, i.e., they are not part of the apparatus of the state, even though they may receive support from governmental sources. This feature differentiates our approach from the economic definitions noted above that exclude organizations from the civil society sector if they receive significant public sector support.

- *Not profit distributing*, i.e., they are not primarily commercial in purpose and do not distribute profits to a set of directors, stockholders, or managers. Civil society organizations can generate profits in the course of their operations, but any such profits must be plowed back into the objectives of the organization. This criterion serves as a proxy for the "public purpose" criterion used in some definitions of civil society, but it does so without having to specify in advance and for all countries what valid "public purposes" are. Rather, it leaves these decisions to the people involved on the theory that if there are people in a country who voluntarily support an organization without hope of receiving a share of any profit the organization generates, this is strong evidence that they must see some public purpose to the organization. This criterion also usefully differentiates civil society organizations from for-profit businesses.

- *Self-governing*, i.e., they have their own mechanisms for internal governance, are able to cease operations on their own authority, and are fundamentally in control of their own affairs.

- *Voluntary*, i.e., membership or participation in them is not legally required or otherwise compulsory. This criterion also helped relate our definition to the concept of public purpose, but one that each country's citizens define for themselves by virtue of their decisions to take part on their own initiative in the organizations affected.

Obviously, like any definition, this one cannot eliminate all "grey areas" or "borderline cases." As these were identified, efforts were made to interpret them in the context of the basic thrust of the definition, and clarifications were issued as appropriate. Thus, for example, when it became clear that the "not profit distributing" criterion, which was included to differentiate civil society organizations from private business firms, as well as from the formally cooperative and mutual enterprises that dominate the banking and insurance industries in many European countries, inadvertently threatened to exclude as well an important class of community-based cooperative institutions serving essentially community development purposes in Latin America and elsewhere in the developing world, language was added to make clear that the latter institutions should be included.

The resulting "structural-operational" definition has now been tested in countries throughout the world and found to be workable in identifying a set of institutions that is sufficiently broad to encompass the great variety of entities commonly considered to be part of the "third" or "civil society" sector in both developed and developing countries, yet sufficiently sharp to be able to distinguish these institutions from those in the other two major sectors—business and government. The result is a definition that encompasses *informal* as well as formal organizations; *religious* as well as *secular* organizations;[9] organizations with paid staff and those staffed entirely by volunteers; and organizations performing essentially *expressive* functions—such as advocacy, cultural expression, community organizing, environmental protection, human rights, religion, representation of interests, and political expression—as well as those performing essentially *service* functions—such as the provision of health, education, or welfare services. While the definition does not embrace individual forms of citizen action such as voting and writing to legislators, it nevertheless embraces most organized forms, including social movements and community based cooperative activities serving fundamentally solidarity objectives, such as the *stokvels*, or revolving credit associations, in Africa. Intentionally excluded, however, are government agencies, private businesses, and commercial cooperatives and mutuals.[10]

For the sake of convenience, we will generally use the term "civil society organizations" or "civil society sector" to refer to the institutions that meet this five-fold structural-operational definition. To be sure, this term is often used in a broader sense to encompass individual citizen activity as well.[11] To emphasize our focus on the more collective and organized forms of civil society, we will generally use the term "civil society organization" or "civil society sector" rather than simply "civil society" to depict the range of social phenomena that is the focus of our attention. This term has gained the widest acceptance internationally to refer to the organizations with which we are concerned. Other terms that will occasionally be used interchangeably to refer to the same set of entities will be "nonprofit sector," "nonprofit organizations," "third sector," and "voluntary organizations." Each of these terms carries its own baggage, but the "civil society" term seems the closest to gaining truly universal usage and has the advantage of avoiding the negative connotations associated with the terms "nonprofit" or "nongovernmental."

**International Classification of Nonprofit Organizations.** As a further aid to clarifying the entities embraced within our project definition, we formulated a classification scheme for differentiating these entities according to their primary activity. To do so, we adopted a method similar to that used for our definition. Beginning with the existing International Standard Industrial Classification (ISIC) used in most international economic statistics, we asked our Local Associates to report how well this classification fit the diverse realities of nonprofit activity in their countries. This input suggested the need to elaborate on the basic ISIC categories in a number of respects to capture the diversity of the civil society sector. Thus, for example, the broad health and human services category of ISIC was broken into a number of subcategories to differentiate better the range of civil society organization activities that exist. So, too, a special "development" category was added to accommodate the "nongovernmental organizations," or NGOs, common in the developing world. These organizations pursue a broad range of development purposes and often utilize an empowerment strategy that blends service and expressive functions.

Out of this process emerged an International Classification of Nonprofit Organizations (ICNPO) that, as shown in Table 2, identifies twelve different categories of nonprofit activity, from recreation and culture to business and professions. Included here are essentially service functions (e.g. the provision of education, health care, or social services) as well as more "expressive" functions (e.g. culture and recreation, religion, advocacy, and environmental protection). Each of these categories in turn is further subdivided into subcategories (see Appendix A for a further specification of the resulting classification system). As will be noted more fully below, this classification structure makes it possible to draw some fairly fine-grained distinctions among the different types of civil society organizations. Like the basic definition, moreover, this classification system has been tested in close to forty countries and found to be both workable and effective.

**Table 2** Fields of nonprofit activity covered by the Johns Hopkins Comparative Nonprofit Sector Project*

| | |
|---|---|
| 1. Culture and recreation | 7.  Civic and advocacy |
| 2. Education and research | 8.  Philanthropic intermediaries |
| 3. Health | 9.  International |
| 4. Social services | 10. Religious congregations |
| 5. Environment | 11. Business and professional, unions |
| 6. Development and housing | 12. Other |

* See Appendix A for additional detail.

**Data sources and methodology**

In order to ensure a reasonable degree of comparability in the basic data generated about the organizations identified above, we developed a data assembly approach that specified a common set of target data items, offered guidance on likely source of such data, and then relied on Local Associates to formulate detailed strategies for generating the needed information in each country. The data items of principal interest to us in the basic descriptive portion of the project that is the focus of this report focused on the overall scope and scale of civil society organization activity and the resources generated to support it. Because it is a notoriously imprecise measure, we devoted little attention to the actual number of organizations and focused instead on variables more indicative of the level of effort these organizations represent. These included the number of full-time equivalent workers, both paid and volunteer; the amount of expenditures; the sources of revenue; and the primary activity.[12]

Broadly speaking, four types of data sources were employed to generate estimates of these key variables:

- Official economic statistics (e.g., employment surveys, population surveys), particularly those that included coverage of civil society organizations, giving, or volunteering. Where the civil society organizations were not separately identified in the data source, as was often the case, a variety of estimating techniques were used to determine the civil society organization share of particular industry aggregates;
- Data assembled by umbrella groups or intermediary associations representing various types of civil society organizations, or industries in which civil society organizations are active;
- Specialized surveys of civil society organizations; and
- Population surveys, focusing particularly on giving and volunteering.

The extent of reliance on these different types of sources varied greatly from country to country and even field to field. Where existing data systems could be tapped to locate relevant information about a class of nonprofit organizations in a country, these were heavily mined. Where such data systems were inadequate or a class of organizations not covered by them, special surveys were carried out. Depending on the legal arrangements and registration systems in place, these surveys began with existing core lists of organizations or with lists that had to be built from the ground up. As the project moved its focus from areas with more developed data systems and more formalized civil society sectors to those with less developed data systems and less formal organizations, the extent of reliance on specially designed, bottom-up surveys naturally expanded. Thus, in Africa and Southeast Asia, detailed "snowball sampling" or "hypernetwork sampling" techniques were used to build profiles of the nonprofit sector from the ground up by going house to house or organization to organization in selected geographic areas, asking respondents about the organizations they belonged to or worked with, and continuing this process until no new organizations were encountered. (For more information on the various data assembly techniques used, see the project Web site: www.jhu.edu/~cnp/research.html.)

**Focus of this report**

Previous publications have summarized the basic descriptive findings of this project with respect to 22 countries in Europe, Asia, North America, and Latin America.[13] The present report extends the analysis to an additional 13 countries, most of them in Africa, the Middle East, and South Asia, which were covered in a special "Phase IIB" of the project.[14] In particular, it provides an overview of the major descriptive findings of the project with respect to the overall size, composition, and financing of the civil society sector in these Phase IIB countries along with the 22 other countries on which we have already reported. This report forms the overview chapter of a book that also contains separate chapters on each of the 13 Phase IIB countries.[15] Subsequent volumes and reports will take up other topics on which the project has focused, such as the social, economic, legal, and historical factors explaining the variations in sector size and character, and the impact that these organizations are having.

**Caveats**

In interpreting the findings, several features of the analysis should be borne in mind:

- Employment data—both paid and volunteer—are expressed in *full-time equivalent* (FTE) terms to make them comparable among countries and organizations. Thus, an organization that employs 20 half-time workers would have the same number of "full-time-equivalent" workers (i.e., 10) as an organization that employs 10 people full-time. Similarly, an organization that employs 10 full-time paid workers would have the same "workforce" as an organization that engages 50 volunteers who work one day a week, or one-fifth time, each.
- Most of the data reported here are unweighted averages in which the values of all countries are counted equally regardless of the size of the country or of its civil society sector. Where aggregate totals are more appropriate (e.g., to report the number of volunteers or paid workers as a share of the total employment in the target countries), weighted figures are used.
- Although data were collected at different *time periods* (1995 for most of the 22 original countries and 1997 or 1998 for the Phase IIB countries), we have attempted to minimize the consequences of the different base years by focusing on the relative size of the nonprofit sector in a country rather than the absolute size, since the relative size is not likely to change much over the two or three year period we are examining. Thus, for example, we measure the workforce of the civil society sector in a country as the percent of the economically active population working for civil society organizations in either paid or volunteer positions.[16]
- As noted above, religious as well as secular organizations were included within the project's definition of the civil society sector, and an effort was made in most countries to capture the activity of both *religious worship organizations* (e.g., churches, synagogues, mosques) and *religiously affiliated service organizations* (e.g., schools, hospitals, homeless shelters). Generally, where a distinction between these two was possible, the affiliated service organizations were included with the other organizations in the relevant service field in which they chiefly operate (e.g., health, education, social services). The organizations primarily engaged in religious worship, by contrast, were assigned to the special category of "religious organizations" (ICNPO Category 10). *Since data on the religious worship organizations could not be gathered on all countries, the discussion here generally excludes the religious worship organizations (but not the religiously affiliated service organizations).* However, where this exclusion affects the results significantly, we also note what difference the inclusion of the

religious worship organizations would make in the countries for which we have data on them.

- The revenues of civil society organizations come from a variety of sources. For the sake of convenience, we have grouped these into three categories: *fees,* which includes private payments for services, membership dues, and investment income; *philanthropy,* which includes individual giving, foundation giving, and corporate giving; and *government* or *public sector support,* which includes grants, contracts, and voucher or third-party payments from all levels of government, including government-financed social security systems that operate as quasi-nongovernmental organizations.
- Unless otherwise noted, *monetary values* are expressed in U.S. dollars at the exchange rate in effect as of the date for which data are reported.
- The number of countries covered varies somewhat by data availability. For example, we have total employment and volunteering data for 35 countries, but have breakdowns by activity field for only 32 of them. Similarly, we have revenue data for 32 countries and complete religious worship data for only 26 countries.

## PRINCIPAL FINDINGS

Five major findings emerge from this work on the scope, structure, financing, and role of the civil society sector in the broad range countries for which we have now assembled data.

## 1. A major economic force

In the first place, in addition to its social and political importance, the civil society sector turns out to be a considerable economic force, accounting for a significant share of national expenditures and employment. More specifically, in just the 35 countries for which we have collected information:

- **A $1.3 trillion industry.** The civil society sector had aggregate expenditures of US$1.3 trillion as of the late 1990s, with religious congregations included. This represents 5.1 percent of the combined gross domestic product (GDP) of these countries (see Table 3).
- **The world's seventh largest economy.** To put these figures into context, if the civil society sector in these countries were a separate national economy, its expenditures would make it the seventh largest economy in the world, ahead of Italy, Brazil, Russia, Spain, and Canada and just behind France and the U.K. (see Table 4).
- **A major employer.** The civil society sector in these 35 countries is also a major employer, with a total workforce of 39.5 million full-time equivalent workers including religious congregations. This means that civil society organizations:

**Table 3** The scale of nonprofit activity, 35 countries, 1995-98

- $1.3 trillion in expenditures
  - 5.1 percent of combined GDP

- 39.5 million FTE workforce, including 21.8 million paid workers and 12.6 million FTE volunteers
  - 4.4 percent of economically active population
  - 46 percent of public sector employment
  - 10 times the employment in the utilities and textile industries in these countries

- 190 million people volunteering
  - 221 volunteers per 1,000 adult population

*Source:* Johns Hopkins Comparative Nonprofit Sector Project

- Employ, on average, 4.4 percent of the economically active population, or an average of almost one out of every 20 economically active persons;
- Employ, in the aggregate, 10 times more people than the utilities and textile industries in these countries, five times more people than the food manufacturing industry, and about 20 percent more people than the transportation industry (see Figure 1).

**Table 4** If the civil society sector were a country...

| Country | GDP (trillion $) |
| --- | --- |
| U.S. | $7.2 |
| Japan | 5.1 |
| China | 2.8 |
| Germany | 2.2 |
| U.K. | 1.4 |
| France | 1.3 |
| **Civil society sector expenditures (35 countries)** | **1.3** |
| Italy | 1.1 |
| Brazil | 0.7 |
| Russia | 0.7 |
| Spain | 0.6 |
| Canada | 0.5 |

• **Paid vs. volunteer workforce.** Of the 39.5 million FTE civil society workers, approximately 16.8 million, or 43 percent, are volunteers and 22.7 million, or 57 percent, are paid workers (Figure 2).[17] This demonstrates the ability of civil society organizations to mobilize sizable amounts of volunteer effort. In fact, the actual number of people involved in the civil society sector exceeds even these numbers since most volunteers work only a few hours a week and even many paid employees work part-time. The actual number of people volunteering for civil society organizations in these 35 countries, for example, exceeds 190 million. This represents over 20 percent of the adult population in these countries.

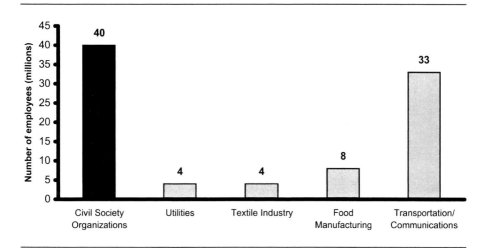

**Figure 1** Civil society organization employment in context, 35 countries

*Source:* Johns Hopkins Comparative Nonprofit Sector Project

## 2. Great variations among countries

While the civil society sector is a sizable force in a wide range of countries, there are considerable differences among countries.

• **Overall variation.** In the first place, countries vary greatly in the overall scale of their civil society workforce. Thus, as Figure 3 makes clear, the civil society sector workforce—volunteer and paid—varies from a high of 14 percent of the economically active population in the Netherlands to a low of 0.4 percent in Mexico.[18]

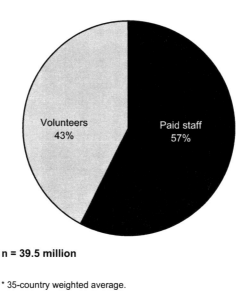

**n = 39.5 million**

* 35-country weighted average.

**Figure 2**  Civil society organization paid vs. volunteer labor, 35 countries*

*Source:* Johns Hopkins Comparative Nonprofit Sector Project

- **Developed vs. developing and transitional countries.** A closer look at Figure 3 suggests that the civil society sector is relatively larger in the more developed countries. In fact, as Figure 4 shows, the civil society organization workforce in the developed countries is proportionally more than three times larger than that in the developing countries (7.4 percent vs. 1.9 percent of the economically active population, respectively).[19] This is so, moreover, even when account is taken of volunteer labor and not just paid employment.

    The relatively limited presence of civil society organizations in the developing countries does not, of course, necessarily mean the absence of helping relationships in these countries. To the contrary, many of these countries have strong traditions of familial, clan, or village networks that perform many of the same functions as civil society institutions. What is more, as Figure 3 also makes clear, there are considerable differences in the scale of civil society activity even among the less developed countries.

- **Variations in reliance on volunteers.** Not only do countries vary considerably in the overall size of their civil society sectors, but also they vary in the extent to which these organizations rely on paid as opposed to volunteer workers.

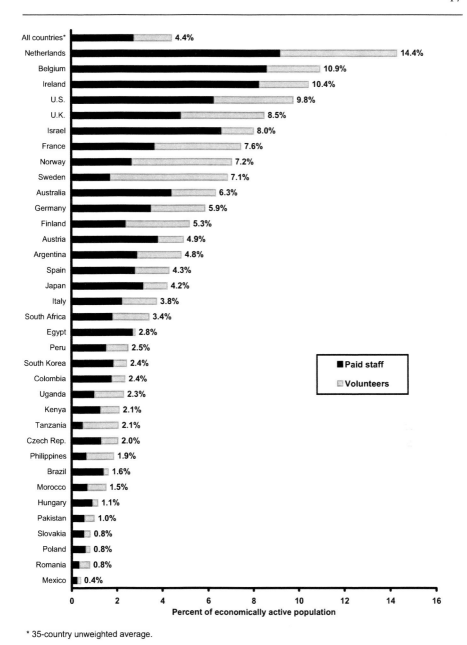

* 35-country unweighted average.

**Figure 3** Civil society organization workforce as share of economically active population, by country

*Source:* Johns Hopkins Comparative Nonprofit Sector Project

Thus, while volunteers comprise 43 percent of the civil society workforce over-all, reliance on volunteers varies considerably among countries—from a low of under 10 percent in Egypt to a high of over 75 percent in Sweden and Tanzania—and averages 38 percent among the countries we have examined.[20]

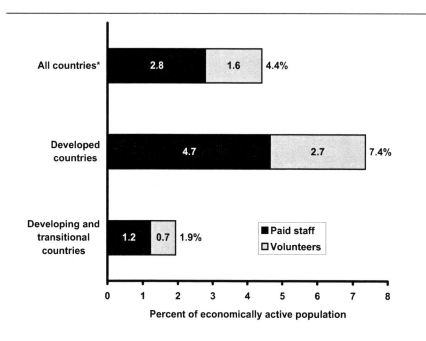

* 35-country unweighted average.

**Figure 4**  Civil society organization workforce as share of economically active population, by level of development

*Source:* Johns Hopkins Comparative Nonprofit Sector Project

Surprisingly, however, no systematic difference exists between developed and developing countries along this dimension.  Both groups of countries have roughly comparable shares of volunteering in their civil society workforce, as Figure 5 also shows.  At the same time, the overall scale of volunteering tends to be higher in the developed countries than in the developing ones. Thus, as Figure 4 shows, volunteers comprise 2.7 percent of the economically active population in the developed countries compared to 0.7 percent in the develop-ing and transitional countries. Since the developed countries also have larger paid nonprofit employment, this suggests that the presence of paid nonprofit employment does not displace volunteers, as is sometimes alleged.  Rather, the larger the paid civil society workforce, other things being equal, the larger the

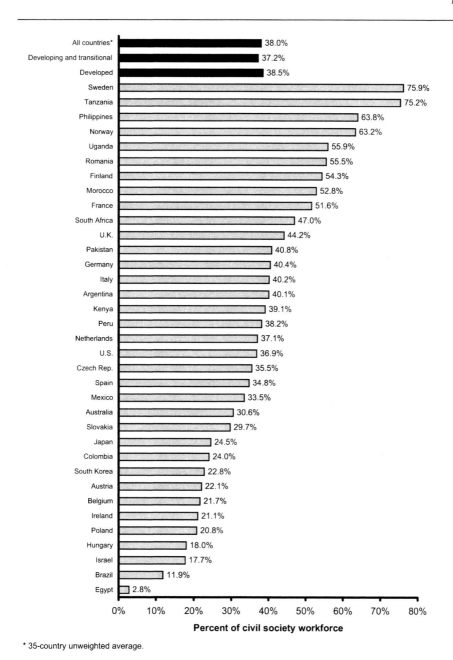

**Figure 5**  Volunteer share of civil society organization workforce, by country

*Source:* Johns Hopkins Comparative Nonprofit Sector Project

volunteer workforce. This is evident in Table 5, which shows the relationship between paid staff and volunteers in our 35 countries.

As this table indicates, of the countries with relatively high levels of civil society organization paid employment, 69 percent also have relatively high levels of civil society organization volunteer employment. By contrast, among the countries with relatively low levels of civil society organization paid staff, 86 percent also have relatively low levels of volunteer employment. In only three cases is low civil society organization paid employment associated with high civil society organization volunteer employment, and all three of these are the Nordic countries (Sweden, Finland, and Norway), where a distinctive pattern of civil society organization development has emerged, as we will see more fully below. This pattern reflects the long history of social movements in these countries coupled with the role that the state has assumed as both a provider and financier of social welfare services, something that is far less in evidence in other countries, including many so-called European "welfare states." To understand this more fully, it is useful to turn from this overview of the size of the civil society sector to an analysis of its composition.

## 3. More than service providers

Civil society organizations are not simply places of employment, of course. What makes them significant are the functions they perform, and these functions are multiple.[21] For one thing, these organizations deliver a variety of human services, from health care and education to social services and community development. While disagreements exist over how "distinctive" civil society organization services are compared to those provided by businesses or governments, these organizations are well known for identifying and addressing unmet needs, for innovating, for delivering services of exceptional quality, and for serving those in greatest need.

But provision of tangible services is only one function of the civil society sector. Also important is the sector's *advocacy* role, its role in identifying unaddressed problems and bringing them to public attention, in protecting basic human rights, and in giving voice to a wide assortment of social, political, environmental, ethnic, and community interests and concerns. The civil society sector is the natural home of social movements and functions as a critical social safety valve, permitting aggrieved groups to bring their concerns to broader public attention and to rally support to improve their circumstances.

Beyond political and policy concerns, the civil society sector also performs a broader *expressive function*, providing the vehicles through which an enormous variety of other sentiments and impulses—artistic, religious, cultural, ethnic, social, recreational—also find expression. Opera companies, symphonies, soccer clubs, churches, synagogues, fraternal societies, book clubs, and girl scouts are just some of the manifestations of this expressive function. Through them, civil society organizations enrich human existence and contribute to the social and cultural vitality of comunity life.

Finally, as noted earlier, these institutions are also important in *community building*, in creating what scholars are increasingly coming to call "social capital," those bonds of trust and reciprocity that seem to be crucial for a democratic polity and a market economy to function effectively. By establishing connections among individuals, involvement in associations teaches norms of cooperation that carry over into political and economic life.

**Table 5** Relationship between civil society organization paid staff and volunteers as a percent of the economically active population, 35 countries

| Paid staff *  Percent of countries | Volunteers*  Percent of countries | | |
|---|---|---|---|
| | below average | above average | Total |
| below average  (n = 13) | 31%[a] | 69%[b] | 100% |
| above average  (n = 22) | 86%[c] | 14%[d] | 100% |
| All  (n = 35) | 66% | 34% | 100% |

\* As percent of economically active population.

Countries represented by percentages in each cell are as follows:

[a] Austria, Israel, Japan, Spain

[b] Argentina, Australia, Belgium, France, Germany, Ireland, Netherlands, U.K., U.S.

[c] Brazil, Colombia, Czech Rep., Egypt, Hungary, Italy, Kenya, Mexico, Morocco, Pakistan, Peru, Philippines, Poland, Romania, Slovakia, South Africa, South Korea, Tanzania, Uganda

[d] Finland, Norway, Sweden

Gauging the extent to which civil society organizations engage in these various activities is difficult because many organizations are often involved in more than one. Nevertheless, it is possible to gain at least a rough first approximation by grouping organizations according to their principal activity and then assessing the level of effort each such activity absorbs.

To simplify this discussion, it is convenient to group the twelve activities identified in our International Classification of Nonprofit Organizations into two broad general categories: (a) *service functions*; and (b) *expressive functions.*

- **Service functions** involve the delivery of direct services such as education, health, housing, economic development promotion, and the like.
- **Expressive functions** involve activities that provide avenues for the expression of cultural, religious, professional, or policy values, interests, and beliefs. Included here are cultural institutions, recreation groups, religious worship organizations, professional associations, advocacy groups, community organizations and the like.

The distinction between expressive and service functions is far from perfect, of course, and many organizations are engaged in both. Nevertheless, the distinction helps clarify the roles that civil society organizations play.[22] In particular:

- **Service functions dominate in scale.** From the evidence available, it appears that the service functions of the civil society sector clearly absorb the lion's share of the activity. Excluding religious worship, for which we have insufficient data, an average of over 60 percent of the total paid and volunteer full-time equivalent workforce of the civil society sector in the 32 countries for which we have activity data work for organizations primarily engaged in service functions (see Figure 6).
- **Education and social services are the dominant service functions.** Among the service activities of the civil society sector, education and social services clearly absorb the largest share, as Figure 6 also shows. Over 40 percent of the nonprofit workforce—paid and volunteer—is engaged in these two service functions on average.
- **Sizable involvement in expressive functions.** While the majority of civil society organization effort goes into organizations primarily engaged in service functions, a significant portion—amounting on average to almost a third of the work force—goes into organizations primarily engaged in expressive functions, as Figure 6 also reveals. The most prominent fields here are culture and recreation and occupational representation. These two account, respectively, for 19 percent and 7 percent of the workforce. By contrast, only 6 percent of the civil society workforce is engaged primarily in civic, advocacy, or environmental activities, though it is likely that a substantial portion of the 8 percent of all civil society organization workers employed in development organizations are also engaged

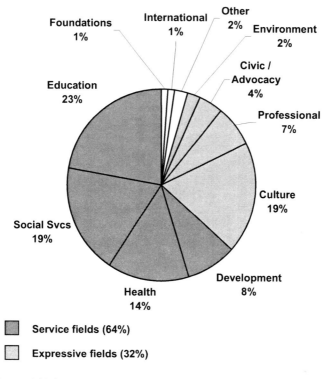

* 32-country unweighted averages.

**Figure 6** Distribution of civil society sector workforce, by field and type of activity*

*Source:* Johns Hopkins Comparative Nonprofit Sector Project

in empowerment activities along with some portion of the workers in other service fields.

- **Volunteer and paid staff roles differ markedly.** Volunteers and paid staff play markedly different roles in the operation of the civil society sector internationally.

    - In the first place, although both volunteers and paid staff are primarily engaged in service functions, paid staff are more heavily involved in these functions than are the volunteers. Thus, while 72 percent of paid staff effort, on average, is devoted to service functions, only 52 percent of the volunteer effort is (see Figure 7).
    - By contrast, only 24 percent of the paid staff time is devoted to the expressive functions compared to 42 percent of the volunteer time. Particularly

noticeable is the role that volunteers play in cultural and recreational activity, which absorbs about 25 percent of all volunteer time.

- Volunteers are also much more actively engaged than paid staff in civic and advocacy activity and environmental protection, which together absorb 10 percent of all volunteer effort. Moreover, if we were to include the 10 percent of all volunteer effort devoted to development organizations, which also often perform an empowerment role, the share of the volunteer effort going into such empowerment functions would rise to 20 percent.

- Even in their service functions, moreover, volunteers appear to concentrate their efforts in different fields than do paid staff. Thus, a sizable 27 percent of all volunteer effort is devoted to organizations providing social services, and 10 percent to organizations primarily engaged in development. The comparable figures for paid staff are 18 percent and 7 percent, respectively. In fact, nearly half of all the work effort in these two fields is supplied by volunteers. Volunteers thus play an especially important role not only in maintaining the nonprofit sector's advocacy functions, but also in helping it maintain its long-standing commitment to social justice and development.

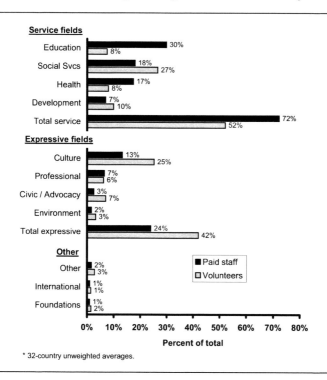

* 32-country unweighted averages.

**Figure 7** Distribution of civil society organization paid and volunteer workforce, by field*

*Source:* Johns Hopkins Comparative Nonprofit Sector Project

- **Inclusion of religious-worship organizations.** This picture of the principal activities of civil society organizations changes only partly when we take account of religious congregations. In the 27 countries for which we have religious congregation workforce data, these organizations engage an average of 8 percent of the total nonprofit workforce, paid and volunteer. Including these workers boosts the expressive share of total nonprofit employment in these countries from 32 percent to 42 percent. As in other expressive fields, volunteers comprise an especially important part of this religious organization workforce. Reflecting this, religious congregations account for an average of only 5 percent of civil society paid staff time in these countries compared to 13 percent of the volunteer time.

- **Variations by country.** As reflected in Figure 8, the service functions of the civil society sector absorb the largest share of the civil society workforce in all but six of 32 countries. What is more, there does not seem to be a marked difference between the developed and the developing countries. In both groups, just over 60 percent of all civil society workers—paid and volunteer—work for service-oriented organizations.

Beyond this aggregate level, however, some interesting variations are apparent in the structure of civil society employment between developed and developing/transitional countries:

- First, in the developed countries, the paid staff tends to focus on service functions while the volunteer staff focuses more heavily on expressive functions. In the developing and transitional countries, however, most volunteer effort goes into service functions. This difference may result from the emergence of government funding of the service functions of the third sector in the developed countries, a point we will return to below. By contrast, in the developing and transitional countries, less public funding is available, and these functions must be handled more fully by volunteers.

- Second, the composition of the service functions performed by civil society organizations differs markedly between these two groups of countries. In particular, organizations engaged in development work absorb a substantially higher proportion of the civil society effort in the developing countries than in the developed ones (11 percent vs. 5 percent). In the African countries, this figure reaches 24 percent of the civil society workforce. This is significant because, as we have noted, these development organizations often have a distinct empowerment orientation that differentiates them from the more assistance-oriented service agencies in fields such as education and health. Coupled with the 33 percent of the civil society workforce occupied in expressive functions, this suggests an especially marked grassroots tilt to civil society activity in these developing regions.

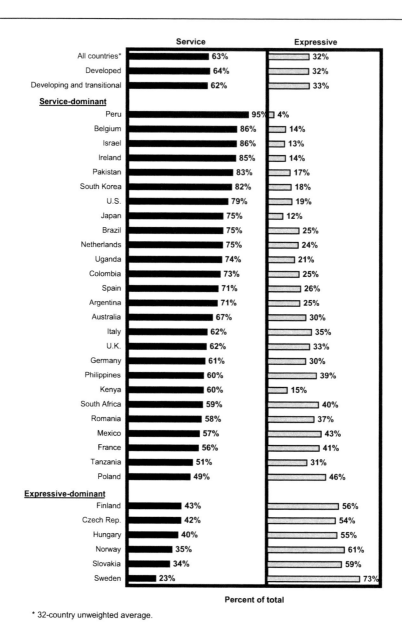

* 32-country unweighted average.

**Figure 8** Civil society organization workforce in service and expressive roles, by country

*Source:* Johns Hopkins Comparative Nonprofit Sector Project

- **Two deviations.** Two other deviations from the general pattern of service dominance among the activities of civil society organizations are evident in the data presented in Figure 8. The first of these relates to the Nordic countries of Finland, Norway, and Sweden. The second relates to the countries of Central and Eastern Europe (the Czech Republic, Hungary, Slovakia, and, to a slightly lesser extent, Poland). In both of these groups of countries organizations primarily engaged in expressive activities absorb a larger share of the civil society workforce than do those engaged in the service functions. As we will note more fully below, the most likely explanation for this is that in both groups of countries the state assumed a dominant position in both the financing and delivery of social welfare services, leaving less room for private, civil society organizations.

  - In Central Europe this was a product of the imposition of a Soviet-style regime in the aftermath of World War II. While this regime concentrated social welfare services in the hands of the state and discouraged, or prohibited, the emergence of independent civil organizations, it did sanction the limited creation of professional and recreational organizations, many of which survived into the post-Communist era.
  - In the Nordic countries, by contrast, a robust network of grassroots labor and social-movement organizations took shape during the late nineteenth century and pushed through a substantial program of social welfare protections financed and delivered by the state. This limited the need for active civil society involvement in service provision but left behind a vibrant heritage of citizen-based civil society activity in advocacy, recreation, and related expressive fields.

  While the structure of the civil society sector in these two groups of countries is similar, however, the scale of the sector differs widely. In particular, the civil society sector in the Central and Eastern European countries remained quite small nearly a decade after the overthrow of the Soviet-type regimes. By contrast, in the Nordic countries, a sizable civil society sector remains in existence today, though it is largely staffed by volunteers and engaged in a variety of cultural, recreational, and expressive functions.

What these findings make clear is that the structure and character of the civil society sector differ markedly from country to country. More than that, these features provide an extraordinary reflection of the broader social, political, and cultural history of a country.

## 4. Not a substitute for government

A fourth key finding of this research relates to the financing of civil society organizations throughout the world. Perhaps the central conclusion here is that private philanthropy accounts for a smaller share of civil society organization revenue than is commonly thought. In particular:

- **Fees are the dominant source of revenue.** In the 32 countries on which revenue data are available,[23] over half (53 percent) of civil society organization income comes, on average, not from private philanthropy but from fees and charges for the services that these organizations provide and the related commercial income they receive from investments and other commercial sources, including dues (see Figure 9).

- **Significant public sector support.** Nor is philanthropy the second largest source of civil society organization revenue internationally. That distinction belongs, rather, to government or the public sector. An average of 35 percent of all civil society organization revenue comes from public sector sources, either through grants and contracts or reimbursement payments made by governmental agencies or quasi-nongovernmental organizations such as publicly financed social security and health agencies.

- **Limited role of private philanthropy.** Private giving from all sources—individuals, foundations, and corporations—accounts for a much smaller 12 percent of total civil society organization revenue in the countries we have examined, or one-third as much as government and less than one-fourth as much as fees and charges.

- **Fee dominance holds in most fields.** This pattern of fee dominance in the revenue base of civil society organizations is fairly consistent among the different fields of activity, although the extent of the dominance does vary. More specifically:

  - *Fees are the largest income source in eight fields.* In six of the 12 fields of civil society organization activity identified in our classification system, (occupational and business organizations, culture, development and housing, foundations, education, and other) fees account for half or more of total revenue, and in two others (environment and civic and advocacy), fees constitute the largest single source of revenue even though they account for something less than half of the total (see Figure 10). This is understandable enough in the cases of occupational and business organizations, and recreation and culture, where membership fees provide important sources of revenue. In the development field, the explanation lies in the inclusion of substantial numbers of housing organizations, many of which collect rents or other payments from occupants. So far as foundations are concerned, over half of their revenue (51 percent) derives from earnings on endowments, which are treated here as fee income. In the case of education organizations, the fees take the form of tuition payments, while for environmental and civic organizations they likely take the form of membership dues.[24]

  - *Public sector-dominant fields.* In two of the 12 major fields of civil society organization action—health and social services—the dominant source of

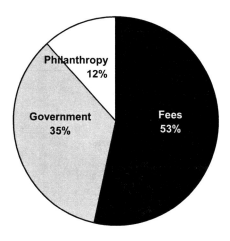

Philanthropy
12%

Government
35%

Fees
53%

\* 32-country unweighted averages.

**Figure 9** Sources of civil society organization revenue\*

*Source:* Johns Hopkins Comparative Nonprofit Sector Project

income is not fees and charges but public sector support. In the case of health organizations, government alone provides over half of the funds. Among social service organizations, government accounts for 44 percent of the funding, fees for 37 percent, and private philanthropy for 19 percent.

- *Private philanthropy-dominant fields.* In only two fields—international assistance and religion—is private philanthropy the dominant source of income, and in one of these—international assistance—government is a very close second (35 percent from government vs. 36 percent from philanthropy).

• **Variations among countries.** As with other facets of the civil society sector, the revenue structure varies considerably among countries, as shown in Figure 11.

- *Fee-dominant countries.* In 22 of the 32 countries, fees are the major source of civil society organization revenue. Interestingly, this pattern is especially marked among the developing countries, which also have the smallest civil society sectors. Thus, the Philippines, Mexico, Kenya, Brazil, Argentina, Colombia, and Peru have the highest levels of reliance on fees and charges. Indeed, for the developing countries as a whole, fees average 62 percent of civil society organization income, compared to only 45 percent for the developed countries. By contrast, government provides only 22 percent of civil society revenue in the developing countries compared to 48 percent in the developed ones. This paradoxical result underlines the dual character of the civil society sector in these countries, with a substantial portion of the sector providing services to a better-off clientele willing and able to pay for the often superior education, health, and related services that civil society organizations can offer; and a smaller development and empowerment-oriented component with relatively limited public sector and fee support.

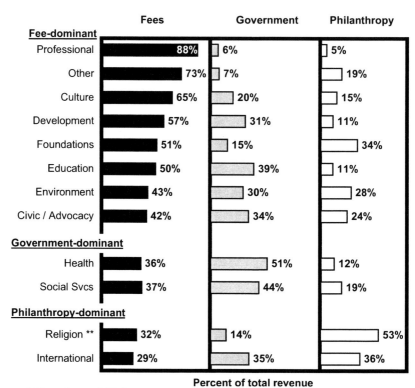

**Figure 10** Sources of civil society organization revenue,* by field

*Source:* Johns Hopkins Comparative Nonprofit Sector Project

- *Government-dominant pattern.* In the remaining countries, public sector support is the largest source of civil society organization revenue, accounting for over 60 percent of the total in four of them. This pattern is especially marked in the developed countries of Western Europe, at least those outside of Scandinavia—such as Ireland, Belgium, Germany, the Netherlands, France, Austria, and the U.K.—as well as in Israel, which followed the same

Western European social democratic tradition. What this makes clear is that outside Scandinavia the Western European "welfare state" tradition actually operated quite differently than has commonly been assumed. Instead of creating a classic welfare state characterized by government provision of a full range of social welfare services, Western European countries actually more often created a widespread welfare *partnership* in which the state finances welfare services but relies heavily on private civil society organizations for their delivery. Far from displacing civil society organizations, the growth of state-financed social welfare actually helped stimulate their growth. Not surprisingly, therefore, these countries have the largest civil society sectors of all the countries we have examined. In short, government emerges from these data as a major source of civil society organization development and growth.

- **Inclusion of volunteering boosts private philanthropy's share of revenue.** The picture of civil society organization revenue portrayed above changes somewhat when the contributions of time represented by volunteers are added to the contributions of money and treated as part of philanthropy.[25]

  - *Aggregate picture.* In the first place, as shown in Figure 12, the inclusion of volunteers in the revenue stream of civil society organizations boosts the average philanthropic share of total revenue from 12 percent to 30 percent. This reflects the fact that contributions of time, even when valued conservatively at the average wage in the fields in which volunteering occurs, are twice as large as contributions of money or material. With volunteer time included, private philanthropy climbs into second place in the revenue base of the civil society sector globally, ahead of public sector payments though still behind fees and charges.
  - *Variations among fields.* The inclusion of volunteer time as part of private philanthropy makes private philanthropy the largest single source of civil society organization income in seven of the 12 fields—religion (73 percent of income from contributions of time and money), international aid (58 percent), civic and advocacy (56 percent), environment (56 percent), foundations (55 percent), recreation and culture (45 percent), and social services (44 percent) (see Figure 13). These data make clear the substantial contribution that volunteer activity makes to the overall operation of the civil society sector, significantly expanding the resources the sector commands and making philanthropy a far more important source of sector support than cash revenue alone would suggest. This is particularly true with regard to the expressive functions such as religion, civic and advocacy activity, and recreation and culture where volunteer input is especially marked; but it holds as well in the service field most closely associated with the sector's social justice mission—social services.

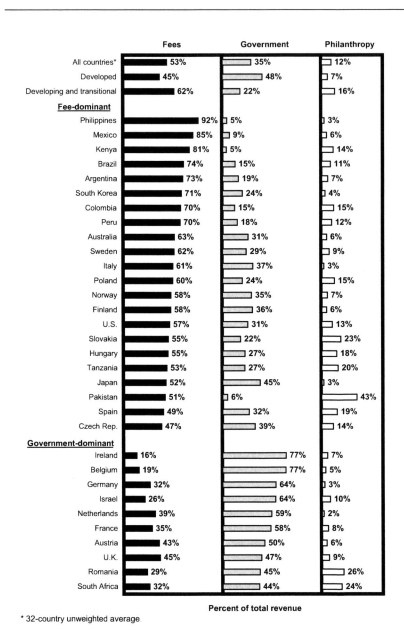

**Figure 11** Sources of civil society organization revenue, by country

*Source:* Johns Hopkins Comparative Nonprofit Sector Project

- *Variations among countries.* The inclusion of volunteer time in the revenue base of the civil society sector also alters the picture of sector finance among countries, though less so. As noted in Figure 14, even with volunteer time included, fees remain the dominant source of civil society organization revenue in eighteen of our 32 countries. What is more, the developing and transitional countries continue to head this list, with an average of 51 percent of their income from fees, compared to only 33 percent among the developed countries. At the same time, the number of countries in which philanthropy becomes the major source of civil society income swells from zero to seven. Especially notable is the sizable role of philanthropy in the Nordic countries of Sweden and Norway once volunteer inputs are included. This reflects the substantial volunteer presence in the workforce of the civil society sector in these countries mentioned earlier. Also notable, however, is the substantial boost that philanthropic support receives from the inclusion of volunteer effort in the three developing countries of Tanzania, Pakistan, and South Africa, with the Philippines not far behind. This suggests the substantial popular base for civil society activity in these countries.

## 5. Regional patterns

From the discussion so far, it should be clear that significant differences exist in the scope, structure, role, and financing of civil society activity in different countries. To an important extent, these differences are country-specific and reflect the particular cultural, social, political, and economic histories of the different countries. At the same time, a number of patterns are also evident that go well beyond the simple distinction between developed and developing countries that we have drawn so far.[26] While any such grouping is necessarily somewhat arbitrary, we find it useful to divide the developed countries we have examined into four regional sub-groups, and to divide the developing and transitional countries into three subgroups plus a fourth "other" category that includes an additional four countries from different regions. Table 6 summarizes the resulting groupings.

The discussion below summarizes some of the salient features of the civil society sector in these clusters of countries and suggests some of the factors that may help explain them. Obviously, this brief overview cannot do justice to the complex set of factors that lies behind the shape of the civil society sector in each country, let alone each cluster, but it can at least suggest the rich insights and questions that can flow from the kind of picture of civil society sector development that our data make possible.

### Developed countries

Among the more developed countries covered by our work, at least four more or less distinct patterns of civil society evolution seem apparent.

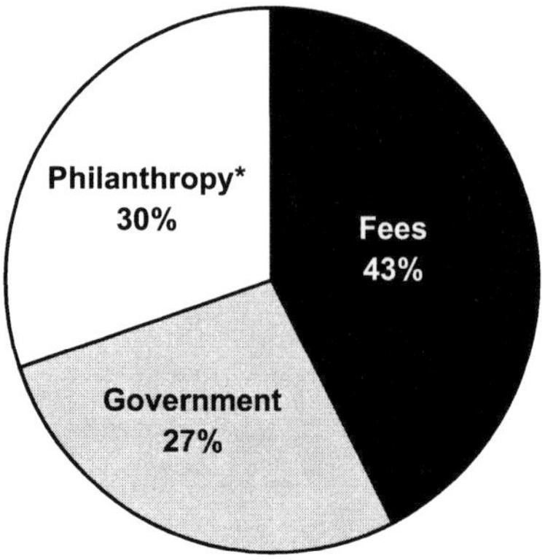

* Includes the value of volunteer time.

**Figure 12**  Sources of civil society organization support (with volunteers), 32 countries

*Source:* Johns Hopkins Comparative Nonprofit Sector Project

**The Anglo-Saxon cluster.** Three countries within our sample—the U.K., the U.S., and Australia—share a high level of economic development and a common historical association with the Anglo-Saxon political and legal tradition. These countries have also historically shared a common approach to social policy characterized by a relatively small, "hands-off" role for the state and significant reliance instead on private, charitable activity. Although government involvement in social welfare provision has expanded in more recent decades—most notably in the U.K. in the aftermath of World War II—these have all been relatively "reluctant" welfare states that have retained a considerable level of reliance on private charity even as public social welfare involvement has grown.

Reflecting this tradition, nonprofit organizations occupy a significant role in these countries. Indeed, as shown in Figure 15, this group of countries boasts the largest average civil society sector workforce of any of the clusters we have identified—an average of 8.2 percent of the economically active population, or nearly double the 35-country average.

A number of other features of the civil society sector in these countries are also notable. One is the sizable volunteer presence, almost twice the all-country average (see Table 7). A second is the heavy focus of these organizations on essentially serv-

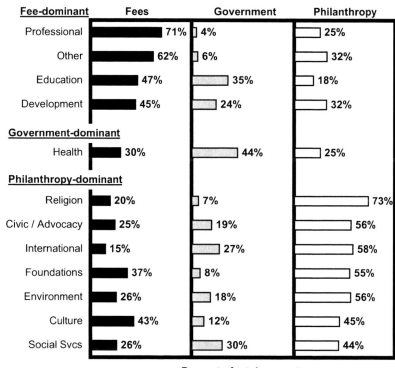

**Figure 13** Sources of civil society organization support, by field, including volunteer time, 32 countries*

*Source:* Johns Hopkins Comparative Nonprofit Sector Project

ice functions (especially among paid staff), though the exact service field in which they concentrate differs from country to country—health services in the U.S. and education in the U.K and Australia.

Finally, the civil society sector in these countries also has a distinctive revenue structure. Contrary to popular mythologies, private charity constitutes a relatively small share of total civil society organization revenue even in these countries—9 percent overall compared to an overall average of 12 percent in our 32-country sample. The largest source of civil society organization income in this set of countries is fees and charges, which are above the all-country average, though the U.K. deviates from this pattern due to its significant departure from the traditional Anglo-Saxon or liberal pattern in the immediate aftermath of World War II when a partial welfare state was

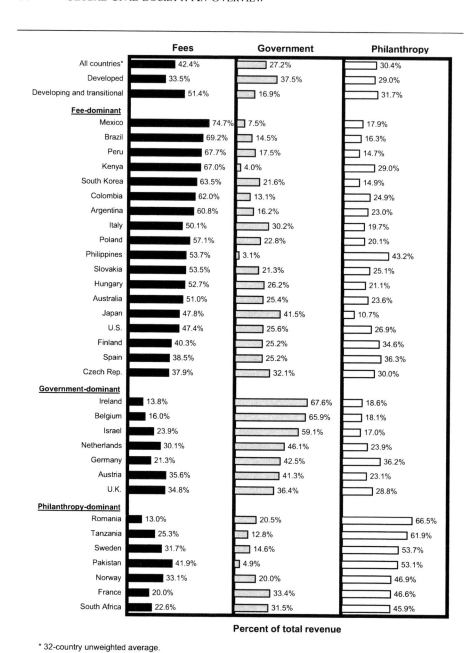

**Figure 14** Sources of civil society organization support (with volunteers), by country

*Source:* Johns Hopkins Comparative Nonprofit Sector Project

created there. The U.K. thus represents a hybrid between the traditional Anglo-Saxon pattern and the continental European one, as we will see more fully below.

The overall contours of civil society sector revenue do not change in these countries when volunteer effort is factored into the equation. Volunteer inputs boost the philanthropy share of income from 9 percent to 26 percent, but philanthropy still lags behind fees and public sector support.

**Nordic welfare states.** A quite different nonprofit reality is evident in the three Scandinavian countries of Finland, Norway, and Sweden. As reflected in Figure 15 and Table 8, the civil society sector in these countries is larger than the 35-country average, but this is largely due to the sizable volunteer workforce that the sector mobilizes. By contrast, the paid nonprofit workforce—at 2.3 percent of the economically active population—is below the 35-country average. This reflects the broad welfare-

**Table 6** Socio-political clusters of countries

| Developed Countries | Developing and Transitional Countries |
|---|---|
| **Anglo-Saxon**<br>Australia<br>U.K.<br>U.S.<br><br>**Nordic Welfare States**<br>Finland<br>Norway<br>Sweden<br><br>**European-Style Welfare Partnerships**<br>Austria<br>Belgium<br>France<br>Germany<br>Ireland<br>Israel<br>Italy<br>Netherlands<br>Spain<br><br>**Asian Industrialized**<br>Japan<br>South Korea | **Latin America**<br>Argentina<br>Brazil<br>Colombia<br>Mexico<br>Peru<br><br>**Africa**<br>Kenya<br>South Africa<br>Tanzania<br>Uganda<br><br>**Central and Eastern Europe**<br>Czech Republic<br>Hungary<br>Poland<br>Romania<br>Slovakia<br><br>**Other Developing**<br>Egypt<br>Morocco<br>Pakistan<br>Philippines |

state policies adopted in these countries early in the twentieth century and the limit-ed reliance placed on private philanthropy and private civil society organizations to deliver basic social and human services. But this does not mean that no civil society sector exists in these countries, as is sometimes supposed. Rather, a rich social move-ment history has long characterized these countries, giving rise to strong advocacy and professional organizations. What is more, voluntary activity has deep roots in Nordic sports and recreational life. This explains the sizable volunteer component of the civil society sector in the Nordic countries (4.1 percent of the economically active population vs. a 35-country average of 1.6 percent). Perhaps because of this also, the

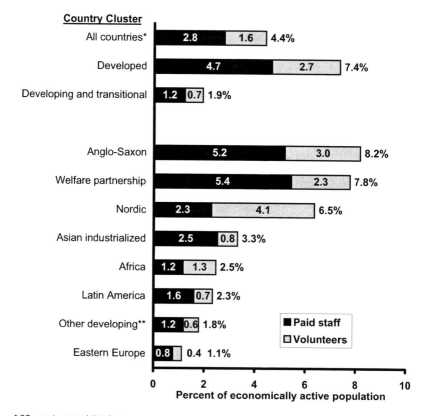

* 35-country unweighted average.
** Egypt, Morocco, Pakistan, and Philippines

**Figure 15** Civil society organization workforce as percent of economically active population, by country cluster

*Source:* Johns Hopkins Comparative Nonprofit Sector Project

revenue structure of the Nordic civil society sector differs considerably from the all-country average, at least with volunteers included. With volunteer inputs excluded, fees, most likely in the form of membership fees, dominate the fiscal structure of the civil society sector in these countries, with government support in second place. Once volunteer inputs are factored in, however, philanthropy—most of it in contributions of time—jumps into first place, accounting for 45 percent of the support. In short, the Nordic pattern features a large civil society sector staffed mainly by volunteers and engaged mostly in expressive rather than service functions.

**Table 7** Anglo-Saxon pattern

| | All countries* | Anglo - Saxon | Australia | U.K. | U.S. |
|---|---|---|---|---|---|
| **Workforce** [1] | | | | | |
| FTE paid | **2.8%** | **5.2%** | 4.4% | 4.8% | 6.3% |
| FTE volunteers | **1.6%** | **3.0%** | 1.9% | 3.6% | 3.5% |
| FTE total | **4.4%** | **8.2%** | 6.3% | 8.5% | 9.8% |
| **Composition of workforce** [2, 4] | | | | | |
| Service | **63.3%** | **69.2%** | 66.8% | 62.0% | 78.8% |
| Expressive | **32.4%** | **27.4%** | 30.3% | 33.2% | 18.8% |
| Other | **4.3%** | **3.4%** | 3.0% | 4.8% | 2.4% |
| **Cash revenues** [3, 4] | | | | | |
| Fees | **53.4%** | **54.6%** | 62.5% | 44.6% | 56.6% |
| Government | **34.9%** | **36.1%** | 31.2% | 46.7% | 30.5% |
| Philanthropy | **11.7%** | **9.3%** | 6.3% | 8.8% | 12.9% |
| **Total support (with volunteers)** [4, 5] | | | | | |
| Fees | **42.4%** | **44.4%** | 51.0% | 34.8% | 47.4% |
| Government | **27.2%** | **29.2%** | 25.4% | 36.4% | 25.6% |
| Philanthropy | **30.4%** | **26.4%** | 23.6% | 28.8% | 26.9% |

* Workforce: 35 countries; composition, revenues, and total support: 32 countries.
1 As percent of economically active population.
2 As percent of total civil society workforce (paid and volunteers).
3 As percent of total cash revenues.
4 Percentages may not add to 100% due to rounding.
5 As percent of total cash and volunteer support.

*Source:* Johns Hopkins Comparative Nonprofit Sector Project

**European-style welfare partnerships**. Elsewhere in Western Europe, the structure, composition, and financing of the civil society sector differ markedly from both the classic Nordic pattern and the Anglo-Saxon one, though this has yet to be fully understood. As reflected in Figure 15 and Table 9, the civil society sector in these countries is generally quite large, averaging 7.8 percent of the economically active population and exceeding 10 percent in three of the countries (Belgium, Ireland, and the Netherlands). Much of this labor force is paid, moreover. In fact, the paid non-profit labor force in these countries is higher on average than in any of the other groupings (5.4 percent of the economically active population vs. 2.8 percent for the 35-country average).

The ability of the civil society sector to support this labor force is due, moreover, to the substantial levels of public sector support available to it. Nearly 60 percent of civil society sector revenue, on average, comes from the public sector in these countries, well above the all-country average. In fact, the public sector accounts for over 50 percent of nonprofit revenue in seven of these countries (Austria, Belgium, France, Germany, Ireland, Israel, and the Netherlands). Consistent with this general pattern, moreover, most of the sizable civil society organization labor force in these countries is engaged in service functions, particularly social welfare services such as education (25 percent), social services (23 percent), and health (20 percent).

These features reflect the distinctive way in which the welfare state evolved in these countries. As in the Nordic countries, popular pressures for social welfare protections led to more extensive, and earlier, government involvement in the social welfare field than in the Anglo-Saxon countries. Though this is commonly viewed as having created a classic "welfare state," in fact, something else seems to have occurred. In large part due to the power of organized religion, particularly the Catholic Church, the state chose, or was persuaded, to funnel social welfare protections extensively through private, voluntary groups, many of them religiously affiliated, rather than delivering the services itself.

The result was an extensive pattern of partnership between the state and the organized civil society sector. In Germany, this partnership was formalized in the principle of "subsidiarity" built into the basic social welfare laws. Under this principle, state authorities are obliged to turn first to the "free welfare associations" to solve social problems. In the Netherlands, a similar pattern emerged out of the conflict between secularists and those committed to value-based education in the early twentieth century. The result was a compromise under which the state financed universal education but through payments to private nonprofit schools, many of them with religious or ideological orientations. This arrangement was then extended to other social benefits, creating a widespread pattern of "pillarization" under which state support was provided to various "pillars" of private institutions. This pattern is also evident in Israel, which was strongly influenced by the Western European social democratic tradition, but which also has an influential religious community as well as a labor movement accustomed to handling important social welfare functions. France presents an interesting variant on the general theme: though it initially followed a path much closer to the Nordic one, the decentralization policies introduced there in the early 1980s led to a significant growth of nonprofit institutions when the local governments found themselves responsible for a variety of human service functions for which they were not staffed and turned to nonprofit organizations for assistance.[27]

The upshot is a distinctive Western European-style welfare partnership pattern characterized by a large civil society sector staffed mostly by paid employees, heavily engaged in service provision, and extensively financed by tax revenues. To be sure, this pattern is not equally present in all of the Western European countries, as the cases of Spain and Italy show.[28] Nevertheless, it is the dominant pattern in this region.

**Table 8** Nordic pattern

| | All countries* | Nordic | Finland | Norway | Sweden |
|---|---|---|---|---|---|
| **Workforce** [1] | | | | | |
| FTE paid | **2.8%** | **2.3%** | 2.4% | 2.7% | 1.7% |
| FTE volunteers | **1.6%** | **4.1%** | 2.8% | 4.4% | 5.1% |
| FTE total | **4.4%** | **6.5%** | 5.3% | 7.2% | 7.1% |
| **Composition of workforce** [2, 4] | | | | | |
| Service | **63.3%** | **33.6%** | 42.6% | 35.5% | 22.6% |
| Expressive | **32.4%** | **63.6%** | 56.4% | 61.1% | 73.2% |
| Other | **4.3%** | **2.9%** | 1.0% | 3.4% | 4.2% |
| **Cash revenues** [3, 4] | | | | | |
| Fees | **53.4%** | **59.4%** | 57.9% | 58.1% | 62.3% |
| Government | **34.9%** | **33.3%** | 36.2% | 35.0% | 28.7% |
| Philanthropy | **11.7%** | **7.3%** | 5.9% | 6.9% | 9.1% |
| **Total support (with volunteers)** [4, 5] | | | | | |
| Fees | **42.4%** | **35.0%** | 40.3% | 33.1% | 31.7% |
| Government | **27.2%** | **19.9%** | 25.2% | 20.0% | 14.6% |
| Philanthropy | **30.4%** | **45.0%** | 34.6% | 46.9% | 53.7% |

\* Workforce: 35 countries; composition, revenues, and total support: 32 countries.
1 As percent of economically active population.
2 As percent of total civil society workforce (paid and volunteers).
3 As percent of total cash revenues.
4 Percentages may not add to 100% due to rounding.
5 As percent of total cash and volunteer support.

*Source:* Johns Hopkins Comparative Nonprofit Sector Project

**The Asian industrialized model.** Japan and South Korea have pursued a different path in the evolution of their civil society sectors as compared with either the Anglo-Saxon or Western European countries, though there are also important differ-

**Table 9** European-style welfare partnership pattern

| | All countries* | Welfare partnership | Austria | Belgium | France | Germany | Ireland | Israel | Italy | Netherlands | Spain |
|---|---|---|---|---|---|---|---|---|---|---|---|
| **Workforce** [1] | | | | | | | | | | | |
| FTE paid | **2.8%** | **5.4%** | 3.8% | 8.6% | 3.7% | 3.5% | 8.3% | 6.6% | 2.3% | 9.2% | 2.8% |
| FTE volunteers | **1.6%** | **2.3%** | 1.1% | 2.3% | 3.7% | 2.3% | 2.1% | 1.4% | 1.5% | 5.1% | 1.5% |
| FTE total | **4.4%** | **7.8%** | 4.9% | 10.9% | 7.6% | 5.9% | 10.4% | 8.0% | 3.8% | 14.4% | 4.3% |
| **Composition of workforce** [2,4] | | | | | | | | | | | |
| Service | **63.3%** | **72.7%** | - | 85.7% | 55.9% | 61.0% | 85.0% | 85.5% | 62.5% | 74.6% | 71.1% |
| Expressive | **32.4%** | **24.5%** | - | 13.7% | 41.1% | 30.0% | 13.5% | 12.8% | 34.8% | 23.9% | 25.9% |
| Other | **4.3%** | **2.9%** | 100.0% | 0.6% | 3.0% | 9.0% | 1.4% | 1.7% | 2.7% | 1.4% | 2.9% |
| **Cash revenues** [3,4] | | | | | | | | | | | |
| Fees | **53.4%** | **35.4%** | 43.5% | 18.6% | 34.6% | 32.3% | 15.8% | 25.8% | 60.6% | 38.6% | 49.0% |
| Government | **34.9%** | **57.6%** | 50.4% | 76.8% | 57.8% | 64.3% | 77.2% | 63.9% | 36.6% | 59.0% | 32.1% |
| Philanthropy | **11.7%** | **7.0%** | 6.1% | 4.7% | 7.5% | 3.4% | 7.0% | 10.2% | 2.8% | 2.4% | 18.8% |
| **Total support (with volunteers)** [4,5] | | | | | | | | | | | |
| Fees | **42.4%** | **27.7%** | 35.6% | 16.0% | 20.0% | 21.3% | 13.8% | 23.9% | 50.1% | 30.1% | 38.5% |
| Government | **27.2%** | **45.7%** | 41.3% | 65.9% | 33.4% | 42.5% | 67.6% | 59.1% | 30.2% | 46.1% | 25.2% |
| Philanthropy | **30.4%** | **26.6%** | 23.1% | 18.1% | 46.6% | 36.2% | 18.6% | 17.0% | 19.7% | 23.9% | 36.3% |

*Source: Johns Hopkins Comparative Nonprofit Sector Project*

* Workforce: 35 countries; composition, revenues, and total support: 32 countries.
1 As percent of economically active population.
2 As percent of total civil society workforce (paid and volunteers).
3 As percent of total cash revenues.
4 Percentages may not add to 100% due to rounding.
5 As percent of total cash and volunteer support.

ences between them in the extent to which they have moved along this path. The civil society sector in these countries is considerably smaller than in the other advanced, industrial societies, engaging only 3.3 percent of the economically active population on average compared to the 35-country average of 4.4 percent (see Figure 15 and Table 10). To the extent that civil society activity exists in these countries, moreover, it is heavily service oriented, much of it in the health and education fields. Reflecting this, fees are the dominant source of civil society organization revenue, accounting for 62 percent on average, though in Japan government support is a close second.

This pattern reflects the distinctive path that industrialization has taken in both of these countries, and in much of Asia more generally. In particular, government has aggressively promoted rapid industrialization while supplying the bare minimum of social protections and generally discouraging, or at least not actively promoting, the development of civil society institutions through which citizens could mobilize effective protests. Although some private charitable organizations took root in these countries, they emerged in large part from the work of Western missionaries, chiefly in the fields of education, health, and social services. The resulting institutions have had to rely heavily on private fees to survive, however, except where government agencies have embraced them to help fulfill public priorities. In these latter situations, however, government bureaucracies have exerted an unusual level of control over the institutions to make sure they adhere to authorized governmental priorities.[29] The result has been a generally small and passive civil society sector, though recent years have witnessed important new stirrings.

### Developing countries

Civil society sector development has taken a somewhat different course in the developing and transitional countries of Africa, South Asia, the Middle East, Latin America, and Central Europe. In some respects, the development of the civil society sector in these countries has been more robust in recent years than in any of the regions covered here, the product of expanding communications technology, frustrations with state-centered approaches to development, and new efforts to empower the rural poor.[30] Despite this, however, civil society organizations still engage a smaller proportion of the economically active populations in these countries than in the more developed regions of the world. One reason for this may be the rural character of these societies and the resulting retention of traditional forms of social assistance relying on clan and family relationships rather than voluntary organization. To the extent such relationships still operate, the need for more institutionalized structures, whether formal or informal, is reduced. So, too, traditional clientelistic systems of social control and modern authoritarian political regimes have often conspired to limit the space available for the development of independent organizations that might threaten the social and political *status quo*. With historically small urban middle class populations and large numbers of marginalized rural poor, these countries have not historically provided a fertile soil for the growth of civil society institutions.

Reflecting these forces, the average size of the civil society sector in the developing countries is well below that of the 35-country average, as we have seen (1.9 percent vs. 4.4 percent of the economically active population), as reflected in Figure 15. Interestingly, the volunteer component of the civil society workforce in these countries is also well below the 35-country average, suggesting that the absence of paid staff hinders rather than helps the mobilization of volunteers.

**Table 10**  Asian Industrialized pattern

| | All countries* | Asian Industrialized | Japan | South Korea |
|---|---|---|---|---|
| **Workforce** [1] | | | | |
| FTE paid | **2.8%** | **2.5%** | 3.2% | 1.9% |
| FTE volunteers | **1.6%** | **0.8%** | 1.0% | 0.6% |
| FTE total | **4.4%** | **3.3%** | 4.2% | 2.4% |
| **Composition of workforce** [2,4] | | | | |
| Service | **63.3%** | **78.4%** | 75.0% | 81.9% |
| Expressive | **32.4%** | **14.9%** | 11.7% | 18.1% |
| Other | **4.3%** | **6.7%** | 13.3% | 0.0% |
| **Cash revenues** [3,4] | | | | |
| Fees | **53.4%** | **61.8%** | 52.1% | 71.4% |
| Government | **34.9%** | **34.8%** | 45.2% | 24.3% |
| Philanthropy | **11.7%** | **3.5%** | 2.6% | 4.4% |
| **Total support (with volunteers)** [4,5] | | | | |
| Fees | **42.4%** | **55.7%** | 47.8% | 63.5% |
| Government | **27.2%** | **31.6%** | 41.5% | 21.6% |
| Philanthropy | **30.4%** | **12.8%** | 10.7% | 14.9% |

\*  Workforce: 35 countries; composition, revenues, and total support: 32 countries.
1 As percent of economically active population.
2 As percent of total civil society workforce (paid and volunteers).
3 As percent of total cash revenues.
4 Percentages may not add to 100% due to rounding.
5 As percent of total cash and volunteer support.

*Source:* Johns Hopkins Comparative Nonprofit Sector Project

Another distinguishing feature of the civil society sector in these countries is the relatively low level of government support available to it (22 percent vs. 35 percent for all countries). These organizations therefore have to depend more heavily on fees and private philanthropy than their counterparts elsewhere, with much of the latter coming from international sources. Even with volunteer effort included, fees remain the dominant source of civil society organization income in these countries.

While the civil society sectors in the developing countries share a number of common features, however, they also differ from each other in important respects. These differences are clearly apparent at the country level, but significant regional variations are also apparent.

**The Latin American model.**  The civil society sector in Latin America is slightly larger than the developing country average, though this is largely due to the inclusion of Argentina, which has a civil society sector on a par with that in many Western European countries (see Table 12). Volunteers play an unusually small part in the workforce of the Latin American civil society sector, accounting for 0.7 percent of the economically active population on average. This may be related to the role that civil society organizations play in this region.  That role, as reflected in the data, is heavily oriented to service functions, and particularly education, which absorbs a third of the total civil society workforce and 44 percent of the paid workers. While some of this represents religious education open to all, a significant portion also reflects elite private education.  Reflecting this, fees and charges constitute an unusually large share (74 percent) of total civil society sector revenue in Latin America.  Even with the value of volunteering included in the revenue base of the region's civil society organizations, fees account for two-thirds of the support.  By contrast, government support—at 15 percent of the revenue—is unusually low, making it difficult for civil society organizations to extend their reach to those in greatest need.  While there is clear evidence of the emergence of advocacy and empowerment-oriented organizations, these institutions maintain a wary coexistence with the more substantial elite-oriented educational institutions and church-related assistance agencies.

**Africa.**  A considerably different civil society reality is evident in the countries of southern and eastern Africa (South Africa, Kenya, Tanzania, and Uganda).  The civil society sector appears quite robust in these countries, engaging as much as 3.4 percent of the economically active population in South Africa and averaging 2.5 percent overall, well above the developing country average (see Table 13). What is more, volunteers comprise over half of the civil society workforce in this region, perhaps reflecting the strong traditions of informal ties along tribal and village lines that have long characterized the region. Also notable is the composition of civil society effort in southern and eastern Africa.  Although over 60 percent of the civil society workforce is engaged in service activities—about on a par with the all-country average—the largest component of this (24 percent of the workforce) works with development organizations, which tend to be more advocacy and empowerment-oriented than traditional charitable service institutions.  Coupled with the 27 percent of other civil society workers engaged in essentially "expressive" functions in Africa, this means that over half of the civil society workforce in Africa has some empowerment or other expressive function, well above the all-country average. This suggests a substantially

larger empowerment character to the African civil society world, perhaps as a byproduct of the struggle for independence from colonial rule or, in the case of South Africa,
against the apartheid regime.

The scale of the African civil society sector remains constrained, however, by the
limited financial support it has available.  Particularly notable, as in other developing
regions, has been the limited availability of public sector funding, which has played
so significant a role in the growth of civil society organizations in the developed
world.  Only 25 percent of civil society organization revenue comes from government
in the African countries, though here gross variations are evident among countries,
with South African organizations recording over 40 percent of their funding from
public sources and Kenyan organizations recording less than 5 percent.  In all these
countries, however, private philanthropy surges into first place as a source of revenue

**Table 11**  Developing and transitional country pattern

|  | All countries* | Developing and transitional |
|---|---|---|
| **Workforce** [1] |  |  |
| FTE paid | 2.8% | 1.2% |
| FTE volunteers | 1.6% | 0.7% |
| FTE total | 4.4% | 1.9% |
| **Composition of workforce** [2, 4] |  |  |
| Service | 63.3% | 62.5% |
| Expressive | 32.4% | 32.7% |
| Other | 4.3% | 4.9% |
| **Cash revenues** [3, 4] |  |  |
| Fees | 53.4% | 62.3% |
| Government | 34.9% | 21.6% |
| Philanthropy | 11.7% | 16.1% |
| **Total support (with volunteers)** [4, 5] |  |  |
| Fees | 42.4% | 51.4% |
| Government | 27.2% | 16.9% |
| Philanthropy | 30.4% | 31.7% |

* Workforce: 35 countries; composition, revenues, and
  total support: 32 countries.
1 As percent of economically active population.
2 As percent of total civil society workforce (paid and volunteers).
3 As percent of total cash revenues.
4 Percentages may not add to 100% due to rounding.
5 As percent of total cash and volunteer support.

*Source:* Johns Hopkins Comparative Nonprofit Sector Project

**Table 12** Latin American pattern

| | All countries* | Developing and transitional | Latin America | Argentina | Brazil | Colombia | Mexico | Peru |
|---|---|---|---|---|---|---|---|---|
| **Workforce** [1] | | | | | | | | |
| FTE paid | **2.8%** | **1.2%** | **1.6%** | 2.9% | 1.4% | 1.8% | 0.3% | 1.5% |
| FTE volunteers | **1.6%** | **0.7%** | **0.7%** | 1.9% | 0.2% | 0.6% | 0.1% | 0.9% |
| FTE total | **4.4%** | **1.9%** | **2.3%** | 4.8% | 1.6% | 2.4% | 0.4% | 2.5% |
| **Composition of workforce** [2,4] | | | | | | | | |
| Service | **63.3%** | **62.5%** | **73.9%** | 70.5% | 74.8% | 72.8% | 56.6% | 94.9% |
| Expressive | **32.4%** | **32.7%** | **24.3%** | 25.3% | 24.6% | 24.7% | 42.6% | 4.3% |
| Other | **4.3%** | **4.9%** | **1.8%** | 4.1% | 0.6% | 2.5% | 0.8% | 0.9% |
| **Cash revenues** [3,4] | | | | | | | | |
| Fees | **53.4%** | **62.3%** | **74.4%** | 73.1% | 73.8% | 70.2% | 85.2% | 69.8% |
| Government | **34.9%** | **21.6%** | **15.3%** | 19.5% | 15.5% | 14.9% | 8.5% | 18.1% |
| Philanthropy | **11.7%** | **16.1%** | **10.3%** | 7.5% | 10.7% | 14.9% | 6.3% | 12.2% |
| **Total support (with volunteers)** [4,5] | | | | | | | | |
| Fees | **42.4%** | **51.4%** | **66.9%** | 60.8% | 69.2% | 62.0% | 74.7% | 67.7% |
| Government | **27.2%** | **16.9%** | **13.8%** | 16.2% | 14.5% | 13.1% | 7.5% | 17.5% |
| Philanthropy | **30.4%** | **31.7%** | **19.4%** | 23.0% | 16.3% | 24.9% | 17.9% | 14.7% |

*Source: Johns Hopkins Comparative Nonprofit Sector Project*

* Workforce: 35 countries; composition, revenues, and total support: 32 countries.
1 As percent of economically active population.
2 As percent of total civil society workforce (paid and volunteers).
3 As percent of total cash revenues.
4 Percentages may not add to 100% due to rounding.
5 As percent of total cash and volunteer support.

once the value of volunteer time is included.  These data suggest the considerable popular support that the civil society sector has generated in southern and eastern Africa and the substantial record of self-help it has helped to foster.

   **Central and Eastern Europe.**  Central and Eastern Europe exhibits yet another pattern of nonprofit sector development, one reflecting the powerful influence on these societies and their civil society sectors of the Soviet-style regimes that came to power in the aftermath of World War II.  Most notable, perhaps, is the extremely small scale of the civil society sector in these countries—engaging only one-fourth as large a proportion of the economically active population as the overall 35-country average. Indeed, as shown in Figure 15, the civil society sector in these countries is smaller than in any of the other regions we examined, including the developing countries of Africa and Latin America. Also notable is the relatively large presence of expressive

**Table 13**  African pattern

| | All countries* | Develop-ing and transi-tional | Africa | Kenya | South Africa | Tanzania | Uganda |
|---|---|---|---|---|---|---|---|
| **Workforce** [1] | | | | | | | |
| FTE paid | **2.8%** | **1.2%** | **1.2%** | 1.3% | 1.8% | 0.5% | 1.0% |
| FTE volunteers | **1.6%** | **0.7%** | **1.3%** | 0.8% | 1.6% | 1.5% | 1.3% |
| FTE total | **4.4%** | **1.9%** | **2.5%** | 2.1% | 3.4% | 2.1% | 2.3% |
| **Composition of workforce** [2,4] | | | | | | | |
| Service | **63.3%** | **62.5%** | **61.0%** | 59.7% | 59.1% | 51.3% | 74.0% |
| Expressive | **32.4%** | **32.7%** | **27.1%** | 15.5% | 40.5% | 31.2% | 21.1% |
| Other | **4.3%** | **4.9%** | **11.9%** | 24.8% | 0.5% | 17.4% | 4.9% |
| **Cash revenues** [3,4] | | | | | | | |
| Fees | **53.4%** | **62.3%** | **55.3%** | 81.0% | 31.7% | 53.1% | - |
| Government | **34.9%** | **21.6%** | **25.3%** | 4.8% | 44.2% | 27.0% | - |
| Philanthropy | **11.7%** | **16.1%** | **19.4%** | 14.2% | 24.2% | 20.0% | - |
| **Total support (with volunteers)** [4,5] | | | | | | | |
| Fees | **42.4%** | **51.4%** | **38.3%** | 67.0% | 22.6% | 25.3% | - |
| Government | **27.2%** | **16.9%** | **16.1%** | 4.0% | 31.5% | 12.8% | - |
| Philanthropy | **30.4%** | **31.7%** | **45.6%** | 29.0% | 45.9% | 61.9% | - |

\*  Workforce: 35 countries; composition, revenues, and total support: 32 countries.
1 As percent of economically active population.
2 As percent of total civil society workforce (paid and volunteers).
3 As percent of total cash revenues.
4 Percentages may not add to 100% due to rounding.
5 As percent of total cash and volunteer support.

*Source:* Johns Hopkins Comparative Nonprofit Sector Project

**Table 14** Central and Eastern European pattern

| | All countries* | Developing and transitional | Eastern Europe | Czech Rep. | Hungary | Poland | Romania | Slovakia |
|---|---|---|---|---|---|---|---|---|
| **Workforce [1]** | | | | | | | | |
| FTE paid | **2.8%** | **1.2%** | **0.8%** | 1.3% | 0.9% | 0.6% | 0.4% | 0.6% |
| FTE volunteers | **1.6%** | **0.7%** | **0.4%** | 0.7% | 0.2% | 0.2% | 0.4% | 0.2% |
| FTE total | **4.4%** | **1.9%** | **1.1%** | 2.0% | 1.1% | 0.8% | 0.8% | 0.8% |
| **Composition of workforce [2, 4]** | | | | | | | | |
| Service | **63.3%** | **62.5%** | **44.7%** | 42.4% | 40.0% | 49.5% | 58.2% | 33.5% |
| Expressive | **32.4%** | **32.7%** | **50.3%** | 54.0% | 55.2% | 46.2% | 36.9% | 58.9% |
| Other | **4.3%** | **4.9%** | **5.0%** | 3.6% | 4.7% | 4.3% | 4.9% | 7.5% |
| **Cash revenues [3, 4]** | | | | | | | | |
| Fees | **53.4%** | **62.3%** | **49.0%** | 46.6% | 54.6% | 60.4% | 28.5% | 54.9% |
| Government | **34.9%** | **21.6%** | **31.5%** | 39.4% | 27.1% | 24.1% | 45.0% | 21.9% |
| Philanthropy | **11.7%** | **16.1%** | **19.5%** | 14.0% | 18.4% | 15.5% | 26.5% | 23.3% |
| **Total support (with volunteers) [4, 5]** | | | | | | | | |
| Fees | **42.4%** | **51.4%** | **42.9%** | 37.9% | 52.7% | 57.1% | 13.0% | 53.5% |
| Government | **27.2%** | **16.9%** | **24.6%** | 32.1% | 26.2% | 22.8% | 20.5% | 21.3% |
| Philanthropy | **30.4%** | **31.7%** | **32.6%** | 30.0% | 21.1% | 20.1% | 66.5% | 25.1% |

\* Workforce: 35 countries; composition, revenues, and total support: 32 countries.
1 As percent of economically active population.
2 As percent of total civil society workforce (paid and volunteers).
3 As percent of total cash revenues.
4 Percentages may not add to 100% due to rounding.
5 As percent of total cash and volunteer support.

*Source:* Johns Hopkins Comparative Nonprofit Sector Project

activity within what little civil society sectors exist in these countries. This is likely a reflection of the social welfare policies of the Soviet-era governments, which relied on direct provision of the most important social services by the "workers' state" and discouraged reliance on private voluntary groups, including those affiliated with religious groups. An embryonic civil society sector was tolerated in these countries, but largely for social, recreational, and professional purposes, and even then at least partly as vehicles for state control. In the aftermath of the collapse of the state socialist regimes, a number of these sanctioned organizations were able to make the transition into nonprofit status, often with the aid of captured state resources (buildings, equipment, and occasionally subsidies), and their relatively sizable presence is reflected in the data.

One particularly ironic byproduct of this peculiar history of civil society development in Central and Eastern Europe is the relatively high level of reliance on philanthropic support on the part of the region's civil society organizations. Ironically, despite its socialist past, philanthropy constitutes a larger share of the revenues of civil society organizations in this region than in any other region (20 percent vs. an all-country average of 12 percent) (see Table 14). One explanation for this may be that when state enterprises were transformed into private firms, they spun off into nonprofit organizations many of the health and recreational services they previously provided to their workers free of cost, but they continued some degree of financial or in-kind support to these activities. Since these state enterprises became private firms, however, this support shows up in our data as private charity.

**Other developing countries.** The remaining four developing countries—Egypt, Morocco, Pakistan, and the Philippines—do not truly form a coherent grouping. To be sure, three of them are heavily Islamic countries with significant recent histories of authoritarian rule. Unfortunately, however, the data available on two of them— Egypt and Morocco—are not sufficient to permit us to draw any but the most tentative conclusions about what this pattern might entail. What does seem clear, at least from the data on Pakistan and the limited data available on Morocco, is that the civil society sector in these countries is relatively small, well below even that in the developing and transitional countries as a whole. This is consistent with a history of authoritarian politics and a cultural tradition that fuses political and religious authority, leaving little room for the emergence of a truly autonomous sphere of organized citizen activity. The Pakistan data suggesting an unusually high involvement of civil society organizations in service activities, and relatively limited involvement in expressive functions, supports this interpretation. Although Egypt seems to deviate from this pattern as reflected in the rather sizable 2.8 percent of the economically active population engaged in civil society activity there, much of this employment represents state workers seconded to civil society social welfare organizations (see Table 15). Until rather recently, in fact, the Egyptian state has maintained a highly distrustful attitude toward its civil society institutions.[31] One other notable feature of the civil society sector in these countries, at least as illustrated by Pakistan, is the unusual level of private philanthropic support that the country's limited civil society organizations receive. Part of this may result from foreign gifts channeled through institutions such

**Table 15** Other developing countries

| | All countries* | Develop-ing and transi-tional | Egypt | Morocco | Pakistan | Philippines |
|---|---|---|---|---|---|---|
| **Workforce** [1] | | | | | | |
| FTE paid | 2.8% | 1.2% | 2.7% | 0.7% | 0.6% | 0.7% |
| FTE volunteers | 1.6% | 0.7% | 0.1% | 0.8% | 0.4% | 1.2% |
| FTE total | 4.4% | 1.9% | 2.8% | 1.5% | 1.0% | 1.9% |
| **Composition of workforce** [2,4] | | | | | | |
| Service | 63.3% | 62.5% | - | - | 82.7% | 59.9% |
| Expressive | 32.4% | 32.7% | - | - | 17.3% | 38.7% |
| Other | 4.3% | 4.9% | - | - | 0.0% | 1.4% |
| **Cash revenues** [3,4] | | | | | | |
| Fees | 53.4% | 62.3% | - | - | 51.1% | 91.6% |
| Government | 34.9% | 21.6% | - | - | 6.0% | 5.2% |
| Philanthropy | 11.7% | 16.1% | - | - | 42.9% | 3.2% |
| **Total support (with volunteers)** [4,5] | | | | | | |
| Fees | 42.4% | 51.4% | - | - | 41.9% | 53.7% |
| Government | 27.2% | 16.9% | - | - | 4.9% | 3.1% |
| Philanthropy | 30.4% | 31.7% | - | - | 53.1% | 43.2% |

* Workforce: 35 countries; composition, revenues, and total support: 32 countries.
1 As percent of economically active population.
2 As percent of total civil society workforce (paid and volunteers).
3 As percent of total cash revenues.
4 Percentages may not add to 100% due to rounding.
5 As percent of total cash and volunteer support.

*Source:* Johns Hopkins Comparative Nonprofit Sector Project

as the Aga Khan Foundation. But part of it likely reflects the strong Islamic tradition of *zakat*, or charitable tithing, which puts a special premium on charitable donations in Islamic society.[32]

The Philippines differs markedly from the other three countries in this grouping. A heavily Catholic country with a long history of colonization by major European powers, the Philippines resembles the Latin American countries examined above. Not surprisingly, therefore, its civil society sector also bears striking resemblance to the Latin American pattern. This is evident in the concentration of the Philippines civil society workforce in services, particularly education (66 percent of paid staff vs. the Latin American average of 44 percent), the prominence of fees and service charges in civil society revenues (92 percent vs. the Latin American average of 74 percent), and the relatively heavy reliance on volunteers in social service provision (84 percent of the total workforce in this field vs. the Latin American average of 56 percent). At the same time, the Philippines civil society sector also reflects the country's recent history of citizen protest against corrupt and authoritarian government as manifested in the above-average civil society workforce engaged in expressive functions.

## CONCLUSIONS AND IMPLICATIONS

The civil society sector is thus a major social and economic force in countries throughout the world at the present time. Once considered to be present only in a handful of countries, these organizations turn out to be a significant presence in virtually every country and region.

This is not to say that important variations are not present in the size, composition, and financing of this set of institutions from country to country. To the contrary, the variations are immense, reflecting the distinctive cultures, traditions, and political histories of the different places. Indeed, one of the strengths of the comparative approach that we have adopted is precisely that it highlights these differences and brings them into better focus. Nevertheless, the ubiquity of civil society organizations remains a central conclusion to emerge from this work.

To say that the civil society sector is a major global force is not, however, to say that it does not face important challenges. To the contrary, the challenges are often enormous. They involve issues of basic visibility and legitimacy, of sustainability, of effectiveness, and of forging the workable partnerships with other sectors that real progress on complex social and economic problems increasingly requires.[33]

To cope with these problems, concerted efforts will be needed. But underlying all such efforts must be a better base of knowledge about this elusive set of institutions. While we harbor no illusions that the work represented here completes this base, we do hope it offers an important foundation on which others can build.

# ENDNOTES

[1] This report is the first chapter of a broader report entitled *Global Civil Society: Dimensions of the Nonprofit Sector*, Volume II, to be published shortly. Ordering information for this broader report is available at: www.jhu.edu/~ccss. The term "global civil society" is used here to refer to the many types of civil society organizations, as defined in the body of this document, that are present, though to varying degrees, in virtually every part of the globe at the present time. It includes both organizations operating across national borders and those operating in particular nations or localities.

[2] Lester M. Salamon, "The Rise of the Nonprofit Sector," *Foreign Affairs*, Vol. 74, No. 3 (July/August 1994).

[3] As one observor has put it: "The fostering of an active civil society is a basic part of the politics of the third way." Anthony Giddens, *The Third Way: The Renewal of Social Democracy* (Cambridge, U.K.: Polity Press, 1998), p. 78.

[4] See, for example: James S. Coleman, *Foundations of Social Theory* (Cambridge: Harvard University Press, 1990), pp. 300-21; Robert Putnam, *Making Democracy Work: Civic Traditions in Modern Italy* (Princeton: Princeton University Press, 1993), pp. 83-116, 163-185.

[5] The System of National Accounts (SNA), the guidance system for international economic statistics, essentially assigns the most important nonprofit institutions to the corporate or government sectors based on their principal source of revenue. See: Lester M. Salamon and Helmut K. Anheier, "Nonprofit Institutions in the Household Sector," in *Household Accounting Experience in Concepts and Compilation*, Vol. I. (New York: United Nations, 2000), pp. 275-99; and Lester M. Salamon, Gabriel Rudney, and Helmut K. Anheier, "Nonprofit Institutions in the System of National Accounts: Country Applications of SNA Guidelines," *Voluntas*, Vol. 4, No. 4 (1993), pp. 486-501.

[6] Quoted in C. Ragin, *The Comparative Method* (Berkeley: University of California Press, 1987), p.1.

[7] For further detail on these alternative definitions and their limitations, see: Lester M. Salamon and Helmut K. Anheier, "In Search of the Nonprofit Sector: The Question of Definitions," in Lester M. Salamon and Helmut K. Anheier, editors, *Defining the Nonprofit Sector: A Cross-national Analysis* (Manchester, U.K.: Manchester University Press, 1997).

[8] For further detail on the derivation of this "structural-operational definition" of the nonprofit sector, see: Lester M. Salamon and Helmut K. Anheier, *Defining the Nonprofit Sector: A Cross-national Analysis* (Manchester, U.K.: Manchester University Press, 1997).

[9] Religious organizations can take at least two different forms: (1) places of religious worship, and (2) service organizations such as schools and hospitals with a religious affiliation. Both of these are included within the project's definition of a civil society organization, though, as noted below, where it was possible to differentiate the two, the religiously affiliated service organizations were grouped together with other service organizations in the relevant field and the religious worship organizations identified separately. Not all countries were able to collect information on the religious worship organizations, however.

[10] Since data on the large mutual and cooperative institutions is fairly readily available, those interested in the broader "social economy" definition, which includes these entities, can easily add them to the data reported here to generate a picture of the broader "social economy." For a discussion of the "social economy" concept, see: Jacques Defourny and Patrick Develtere, "The Social Economy: The Worldwide Making of a Third Sector," in J. Defourny, P. Develtere, and B. Foneneau, *L'economie sociale au Nord et au Sud* (DeBoeck, 1999).

[11] For an illustration of the confusion attending the "civil society" concept, see: Alan Fowler, "Civil Society Research Findings from a Global Perspective: A Case for Redressing Bias, Asymmetry, and Bifurcation," *Voluntas*, Vol. 13, No. 3, 287-300 (September 2002). Although claiming to use a different concept than the one adopted here, Fowler defines civil society in terms quite consistent with the definition adopted in this project—i.e., "an arena of voluntary formal and informal collective citizen engagement distinct from families, state, and profit-seeking institutions." The emphasis on "collective" engagement in this definition is similar to our focus on organizations.

[12] Other components of the project examined additional key facets of the civil society sector in the target countries such as the legal framework, the history, religious and cultural traditions, and the policy context.

[13] For a summary of the results of Phase I of project work, focusing on eight countries, see: Lester M. Salamon and Helmut K. Anheier, *The Emerging Sector: An Overview* (Baltimore, MD: Johns Hopkins Institute for Policy Studies, 1994), republished as *The Emerging Nonprofit Sector,* Vol. 1 in the Johns Hopkins Nonprofit Sector Series (Manchester: Manchester University Press, 1996). More detailed results are available in a series of books published in the Johns Hopkins Nonprofit Sector Series by Manchester University Press. Results of the second phase of project work, covering 22 countries, can be found in: Lester M. Salamon, Helmut K. Anheier, Regina List, Wojciech Sokolowski, Stefan Toepler, and Associates, *Global Civil Society: Dimensions of the Nonprofit Sector* (Baltimore: Johns Hopkins Center for Civil Society Studies, 1999). For a complete list of the products of the Johns Hopkins Comparative Nonprofit Sector Project, please contact the Center for Civil Society Studies as noted on the back cover. Project results are also available online at: www.jhu.edu/~cnp/research.html.

[14] In addition to these 13 countries for which data are reported here, Phase IIB also covered three other countries—India, Lebanon, and Thailand—for which data were not available as this report went to press.

[15] For details on this book, see the Center for Civil Society Studies Web site at: www.jhu.edu/~ccss/pubs/.

[16] Readers of our previous reports will note that the basis of comparison used here differs slightly from that used previously. In particular, we compare nonprofit employment here to the *economically active population* in the countries covered rather than to the *nonagricultural workforce* as in previous reports. This change was made necessary because of the huge size of the agricultural workforce, the large informal economy, and the resulting relatively small size of the formally recorded "workforce" in many of the countries now covered by the project. In India, for example, no more than 10 percent of the economically active population—i.e., the population of working age that is able to work—is recorded in government documents as part of the formal "labor force." This change in the base of the percentages means that the relative size of the nonprofit sector reported here appears lower than that reported in previous reports for some of the countries covered. This is so because the "economically active population" is generally larger than the "nonagricultural labor force," the base used for the earlier figures. "Economically active population" is essentially the population of working age that is not institutionalized or otherwise unavailable for productive work, whether they are formally employed, self-employed, producing for their own consumption, or looking for work. See: International Labor Organization, *Current International Recommendations on Labour Statistics* (Geneva: International Labour Organization, 1988).

[17] This is a weighted average considering the aggregate number of paid and volunteer workers (including those in religious worship organizations). As will be noted more fully below, the unweighted average differs slightly because the countries with the larger nonprofit sectors also tend to have higher numbers of volunteers. The unweighted average volunteer share of nonprofit employment is thus 38 percent.

[18] As noted earlier, the figure reported here for the Netherlands appears lower than in our earlier publications. This is not due to any change in the relative size of the civil society workforce in The Netherlands, but rather to our decision to compare this workforce to the "economically active population" rather than the "nonagricultural workforce" as before. For an explanation of this decision, see note 16 above.

[19] The distinction between developed and developing countries here is based on the classification found in the World Bank's *World Development Report* (Oxford University Press, 2001), which in turn is based on per capita gross national product (GNP). All countries classified as "high income" (1999 per capita GNP of $9,266 or more) are considered here as "developed," whereas, all countries falling below that level are classified as "developing" and "transitional." Specifically, the developed country group includes the following 16 countries: Australia, Austria, Belgium, Finland, France, Germany, Ireland, Israel, Italy, Japan, the Netherlands, Norway, Spain, Sweden, the U.K., and the U.S. The following 19 countries are included in the developing and transitional group: Argentina, Brazil, Colombia, the Czech Republic, Egypt, Hungary, Kenya, Mexico, Morocco, Pakistan, Peru, the Philippines, Poland, Romania, Slovakia, South Africa, South Korea, Tanzania, and Uganda.

[20] The difference between the two measures of the volunteer share of the nonprofit workforce reported here is that the 43 percent is a weighted average, and the 38 percent is an unweighted average. For further debate on this distinction, see page 12.

[21] For an elaboration on these functions, see: Lester M. Salamon, *America's Nonprofit Sector: A Primer.* Second Edition. (New York: The Foundation Center, 1999), pp. 15-17.

[22] To some extent this distinction may correspond to that sometimes drawn between civil society organizations that are primarily agencies of assistance, and those that are fundamentally agencies of empowerment seeking to change the relations of power thought to create the need for assistance. See, for example: Julie Fisher, *The Road from Rio: Sustainable Development and the Nongovernmental Movement in the Third World.* (Westport, CN: Praeger, 1993); John P. Lewis, *Strengthening the Poor: What Have We Learned* (New Brunswick: Transaction Books, 1988).

[23] Revenue data could not be collected in Egypt, Morocco, and Uganda.

[24] Some of these dues could reasonably be considered philanthropic contributions on the part of members committed to the values being promoted by the organizations, though they are treated here as dues.

[25] For purposes of these calculations, volunteer time is valued at the average wage in the respective country in the fields in which volunteering takes place.

[26] For an earlier effort to identify and explain patterns of third sector development among countries, see: Lester M. Salamon and Helmut K. Anheier, "Social Origins of Civil Society: Explaining the Nonprofit Sector Cross-Nationally." *Voluntas,* Vol. 9, No. 3 (1998), pp. 213-248. For a more complete account, see Lester M. Salamon, S. Wojciech Sokolowski, and Helmut K. Anheier, *Social Origins of Civil Society,* (New York: Cambridge University Press, forthcoming).

[27] For further detail on these cases, see: Salamon et al., *Global Civil Society: Dimensions of the Nonprofit Sector* (Baltimore: Johns Hopkins Center for Civil Society Studies, 1999); Anheier and Zimmer, *The Nonprofit Sector in Germany* (Manchester University Press, 1997); Archambault, *The Nonprofit Sector in France* (Manchester University Press, 1997); Burger, Dekker, van der Ploeg, and van Veen, *Defining the Nonprofit Sector: The Netherlands* (Baltimore: Johns Hopkins Institute for Policy Studies, 1997); and Kramer, *Voluntary Agencies in the Welfare State* (Berkeley: University of California Press, 1981).

[28] One possible explanation for these deviations is the greater power that the state secured vis-à-vis the church in these two countries. For further exploration of these points, see: Salamon and Sokolowski, *Social Origins of Civil Society* (New York: Cambridge University Press, forthcoming).

[29] Takeyoshi Amenomori, "Japan," in Lester M. Salamon and Helmut K. Anheier, eds., *Defining the Nonprofit Sector.* (Manchester, U.K.: Manchester University Press, 1997), pp. 188-214; Tadashi Yamamoto, "The State and the Nonprofit Sector in Japan," in Tadashi Yamamoto, editor. *The Nonprofit Sector in Japan.* No. 7 in the Johns Hopkins Nonprofit Sector Series edited by Lester M. Salamon and Helmut K. Anheier. (Manchester, U.K.: Manchester University Press, 1998), pp. 119-144.

[30] See, for example, Fisher, *The Road from Rio* (Westport: Praeger, 1993).

[31] See, for example: Amani Kandil, "The Nonprofit Sector in Egypt," in Helmut K. Anheier and Lester M. Salamon, editors, *The Nonprofit Sector in the Developing World,* (Manchester, U.K.: Manchester University Press, 1998), pp. 149-51.

[32] Amani Kandil, *Civil Society in the Islamic World.* (Washington: CIVICUS, 1995).

[33] For further elaboration on these challenges, see: Lester M. Salamon, "The Third Sector in Global Perspectives," *Building Democracy from the Grassroots* (Washington, D.C.: The Inter-American Foundation, 2001).

# APPENDIX A

**Table A.1**   International Classification of Nonprofit Organizations (ICNPO): major groups and subgroups

GROUP 1: CULTURE AND RECREATION
  1 100  Culture and Arts
  1 200  Sports
  1 300  Other Recreation and Social Clubs

GROUP 2: EDUCATION AND RESEARCH
  2 100  Primary and Secondary Education
  2 200  Higher Education
  2 300  Other Education
  2 400  Research

GROUP 3: HEALTH
  3 100  Hospitals and Rehabilitation
  3 200  Nursing Homes
  3 300  Mental Health and Crisis Intervention
  3 400  Other Health Services

GROUP 4: SOCIAL SERVICES
  4 100  Social Services
  4 200  Emergency and Relief
  4 300  Income Support and Maintenance

GROUP 5: ENVIRONMENT
  5 100  Environment
  5 200  Animal Protection

GROUP 6: DEVELOPMENT AND HOUSING
  6 100  Economic, Social and Community Development
  6 200  Housing
  6 300  Employment and Training

GROUP 7: LAW, ADVOCACY AND POLITICS
  7 100  Civic and Advocacy Organizations
  7 200  Law and Legal Services
  7 300  Political Organizations

GROUP 8: PHILANTHROPIC INTERMEDIARIES AND VOLUNTARISM PROMOTION

GROUP 9: INTERNATIONAL

GROUP 10: RELIGION

GROUP 11: BUSINESS AND PROFESSIONAL ASSOCIATIONS, UNIONS

GROUP 12: [NOT ELSEWHERE CLASSIFIED]

# APPENDIX B

## Table B.1  Civil society sector FTE paid employment, by field, 35 countries

| | Culture | Education | Health | Social Svcs | Environment | Development | Civic / Advocacy | Foundations | International | Professional | Other | Total (thousands) |
|---|---|---|---|---|---|---|---|---|---|---|---|---|
| | Percent* of total civil society paid employment | | | | | | | | | | | |
| Argentina | 15.1 | 41.2 | 13.4 | 10.7 | 0.3 | 5.7 | 0.4 | 0.2 | 1.3 | 6.8 | 4.9 | 395.3 |
| Australia | 16.4 | 23.3 | 18.6 | 20.1 | 0.5 | 10.8 | 3.2 | 0.1 | 0.2 | 4.3 | 2.6 | 402.6 |
| Austria | 8.4 | 8.9 | 11.6 | 64.0 | 0.4 | 0.0 | 4.5 | 0.0 | 0.8 | 1.4 | 0.0 | 143.6 |
| Belgium | 4.9 | 38.8 | 30.4 | 13.8 | 0.5 | 9.9 | 0.4 | 0.2 | 0.2 | 0.9 | 0.0 | 357.8 |
| Brazil | 17.0 | 36.9 | 17.8 | 16.4 | 0.2 | 1.1 | 0.6 | 0.0 | 0.4 | 9.6 | 0.0 | 1034.6 |
| Colombia | 9.4 | 26.1 | 17.5 | 14.6 | 0.8 | 13.1 | 1.3 | 0.9 | 0.1 | 15.1 | 1.2 | 286.9 |
| Czech Rep. | 31.0 | 14.6 | 13.6 | 11.2 | 3.7 | 7.4 | 3.1 | 2.0 | 1.1 | 12.3 | 0.0 | 74.2 |
| Egypt | 0.0 | 0.0 | 0.0 | 0.0 | 0.0 | 0.0 | 0.0 | 0.0 | 0.0 | 0.0 | 0.0 | 611.9 |
| Finland | 14.2 | 25.0 | 23.0 | 17.8 | 1.0 | 2.4 | 8.7 | 0.0 | 0.3 | 7.2 | 0.3 | 62.8 |
| France | 12.1 | 20.7 | 15.5 | 39.7 | 1.0 | 5.5 | 1.9 | 0.0 | 1.8 | 1.8 | 0.0 | 959.8 |
| Germany | 5.4 | 11.7 | 30.6 | 38.8 | 0.8 | 6.1 | 1.6 | 0.4 | 0.7 | 3.9 | 0.0 | 1440.9 |
| Hungary | 38.1 | 10.0 | 4.5 | 11.1 | 2.0 | 13.2 | 1.0 | 3.3 | 0.8 | 16.1 | 0.0 | 44.9 |
| Ireland | 6.0 | 53.7 | 27.6 | 4.5 | 0.9 | 4.3 | 0.4 | 0.1 | 0.3 | 2.2 | 0.0 | 118.7 |
| Israel | 5.9 | 50.3 | 27.0 | 10.9 | 0.8 | 1.0 | 0.4 | 2.0 | 0.1 | 1.8 | 0.0 | 145.4 |
| Italy | 11.9 | 20.3 | 21.6 | 27.5 | 0.5 | 5.1 | 2.0 | 0.1 | 0.2 | 8.9 | 1.8 | 568.5 |
| Japan | 3.1 | 22.5 | 47.1 | 16.6 | 0.4 | 0.3 | 0.2 | 0.2 | 0.4 | 5.0 | 4.3 | 2140.1 |
| Kenya | 4.1 | 12.0 | 4.2 | 22.4 | 4.5 | 19.3 | 5.4 | 0.4 | 0.0 | 1.1 | 26.6 | 174.9 |
| Mexico | 7.7 | 43.2 | 8.1 | 8.7 | 0.7 | 0.5 | 0.3 | 0.3 | 0.0 | 30.5 | 0.0 | 93.8 |
| Morocco | 0.0 | 0.0 | 0.0 | 0.0 | 0.0 | 0.0 | 0.0 | 0.0 | 0.0 | 0.0 | 0.0 | 74.5 |
| Netherlands | 4.1 | 27.4 | 42.6 | 18.9 | 1.0 | 2.5 | 0.6 | 0.4 | 0.6 | 1.9 | 0.0 | 661.7 |
| Norway | 13.3 | 25.9 | 10.3 | 25.9 | 0.2 | 2.6 | 2.9 | 0.2 | 1.8 | 16.8 | 0.1 | 60.0 |
| Pakistan | 0.3 | 71.9 | 11.3 | 3.0 | 0.0 | 7.6 | 5.1 | 0.0 | 0.0 | 0.9 | 0.0 | 261.8 |
| Peru | 4.0 | 72.7 | 4.1 | 1.2 | 0.6 | 14.2 | 0.8 | 1.4 | 0.0 | 1.1 | 0.0 | 129.8 |
| Philippines | 2.1 | 65.7 | 2.3 | 2.8 | 2.8 | 9.5 | 0.8 | 2.0 | 0.7 | 11.3 | 0.0 | 187.3 |
| Poland | 31.6 | 23.7 | 7.2 | 17.3 | 1.8 | 1.1 | 0.9 | 0.4 | 0.7 | 11.5 | 3.7 | 122.5 |
| Romania | 34.0 | 17.9 | 13.1 | 20.7 | 0.7 | 3.6 | 4.4 | 0.8 | 1.3 | 3.6 | 0.0 | 37.4 |
| Slovakia | 36.7 | 28.5 | 1.9 | 5.2 | 6.8 | 1.1 | 2.9 | 4.9 | 0.9 | 10.4 | 0.8 | 16.2 |
| South Africa | 9.4 | 8.6 | 13.7 | 31.4 | 7.8 | 19.0 | 8.5 | 0.5 | 0.0 | 1.1 | 0.0 | 298.2 |
| South Korea | 4.9 | 52.0 | 26.8 | 9.3 | 0.0 | 0.0 | 2.7 | 0.0 | 0.0 | 4.3 | 0.0 | 413.3 |
| Spain | 11.8 | 25.1 | 12.2 | 31.8 | 0.3 | 11.2 | 3.4 | 0.1 | 2.0 | 1.8 | 0.3 | 475.2 |
| Sweden | 26.9 | 20.8 | 3.3 | 17.8 | 2.0 | 6.1 | 3.7 | 0.6 | 2.7 | 14.8 | 1.1 | 82.6 |
| Tanzania | 9.0 | 15.9 | 14.0 | 11.2 | 8.8 | 12.2 | 7.1 | 7.9 | 4.3 | 3.4 | 6.0 | 82.0 |
| Uganda | 6.2 | 9.6 | 26.3 | 21.3 | 1.8 | 21.0 | 3.1 | 2.6 | 7.3 | 0.8 | 0.0 | 102.7 |
| U.K. | 24.5 | 41.5 | 4.3 | 13.1 | 1.3 | 7.6 | 0.7 | 0.7 | 3.8 | 2.6 | 0.0 | 1415.7 |
| U.S. | 7.3 | 21.5 | 46.3 | 13.5 | 0.0 | 6.3 | 1.8 | 0.3 | 0.0 | 2.9 | 0.0 | 8554.9 |

* Percentages add to 100% across fields.

Source: Johns Hopkins Comparative Nonprofit Sector Project

## Table B.2  Civil society sector FTE volunteering, by field, 35 countries

| | Culture | Education | Health | Social Svcs | Environment | Development | Civic / Advocacy | Foundations | International | Professional | Other | Total (thousands) |
|---|---|---|---|---|---|---|---|---|---|---|---|---|
| | | | | | Percent* of total civil society volunteering | | | | | | | |
| Argentina | 11.9 | 17.1 | 4.4 | 17.8 | 3.4 | 30.6 | 3.8 | 0.0 | 0.0 | 10.3 | 0.7 | 264.1 |
| Australia | 37.0 | 5.8 | 6.4 | 31.6 | 3.6 | 9.4 | 2.1 | 0.4 | 0.7 | 1.0 | 2.0 | 177.1 |
| Austria | | | | | | n / a | | | | | | 40.7 |
| Belgium | 33.7 | 0.6 | 0.4 | 55.9 | 0.6 | 2.5 | 1.0 | 0.7 | 1.0 | 3.5 | 0.0 | 99.1 |
| Brazil | 1.1 | 21.3 | 15.6 | 40.0 | 0.0 | 17.5 | 1.4 | 0.0 | 0.0 | 0.9 | 2.1 | 139.2 |
| Colombia | 1.8 | 1.8 | 8.4 | 31.6 | 0.6 | 35.6 | 2.4 | 3.3 | 0.0 | 14.3 | 0.1 | 90.8 |
| Czech Rep. | 44.4 | 3.3 | 8.9 | 16.7 | 10.4 | 5.6 | 4.4 | 2.5 | 2.0 | 1.7 | 0.0 | 40.9 |
| Egypt | | | | | | n / a | | | | | | 17.3 |
| Finland | 48.2 | 1.7 | 4.7 | 13.6 | 0.5 | 1.0 | 23.6 | 0.3 | 0.5 | 5.4 | 0.5 | 74.8 |
| France | 46.7 | 8.9 | 3.4 | 15.7 | 8.7 | 4.0 | 1.8 | 1.1 | 3.0 | 6.6 | 0.0 | 1021.7 |
| Germany | 40.9 | 1.5 | 8.7 | 10.1 | 5.7 | 2.0 | 5.7 | 2.0 | 2.9 | 4.8 | 15.8 | 978.1 |
| Hungary | 30.8 | 4.1 | 5.5 | 33.5 | 2.9 | 2.6 | 8.5 | 5.5 | 2.3 | 4.2 | 0.0 | 9.9 |
| Ireland | 27.2 | 2.8 | 7.4 | 45.1 | 0.7 | 10.9 | 0.7 | 2.8 | 0.7 | 0.0 | 1.6 | 31.7 |
| Israel | 21.5 | 0.3 | 28.4 | 40.0 | 0.0 | 0.0 | 9.2 | 0.0 | 0.0 | 0.6 | 0.0 | 31.3 |
| Italy | 41.7 | 6.5 | 12.8 | 23.9 | 2.3 | 1.4 | 4.6 | 1.9 | 1.2 | 3.3 | 0.5 | 381.6 |
| Japan | 12.9 | 6.1 | 7.2 | 19.4 | 1.6 | 6.7 | 1.5 | 3.7 | 5.4 | 5.0 | 30.5 | 695.1 |
| Kenya | 5.8 | 8.9 | 19.4 | 12.7 | 3.2 | 21.4 | 5.0 | 0.1 | 0.0 | 2.1 | 21.2 | 112.4 |
| Mexico | 3.8 | 5.7 | 9.2 | 31.3 | 3.9 | 2.7 | 1.8 | 1.7 | 0.0 | 39.7 | 0.0 | 47.2 |
| Morocco | | | | | | n / a | | | | | | 83.4 |
| Netherlands | 39.4 | 15.8 | 7.4 | 22.7 | 3.9 | 0.2 | 6.9 | 0.0 | 2.2 | 1.6 | 0.0 | 390.1 |
| Norway | 57.4 | 2.7 | 3.5 | 7.0 | 0.8 | 5.3 | 8.2 | 0.2 | 3.5 | 10.9 | 0.5 | 103.0 |
| Pakistan | 12.3 | 34.4 | 9.1 | 15.3 | 0.8 | 8.0 | 17.2 | 0.0 | 0.0 | 2.8 | 0.0 | 180.8 |
| Peru | 0.1 | 0.5 | 0.1 | 98.5 | 0.2 | 0.1 | 0.0 | 0.0 | 0.0 | 0.6 | 0.0 | 80.1 |
| Philippines | 7.6 | 10.5 | 1.8 | 8.1 | 1.7 | 28.0 | 2.2 | 0.4 | 0.2 | 39.5 | 0.0 | 330.3 |
| Poland | 36.9 | 16.5 | 4.7 | 28.2 | 1.2 | 0.6 | 1.4 | 0.3 | 2.0 | 8.2 | 0.1 | 32.1 |
| Romania | 24.2 | 12.8 | 4.8 | 41.5 | 3.4 | 1.4 | 3.3 | 1.1 | 6.1 | 1.5 | 0.0 | 46.5 |
| Slovakia | 37.8 | 1.4 | 1.9 | 21.8 | 14.2 | 1.1 | 5.8 | 7.1 | 1.0 | 6.1 | 1.8 | 6.9 |
| South Africa | 26.8 | 2.1 | 5.9 | 19.1 | 3.7 | 16.6 | 24.4 | 0.3 | 0.1 | 1.0 | 0.0 | 264.3 |
| South Korea | 4.9 | 1.7 | 22.5 | 36.5 | 0.0 | 0.0 | 34.2 | 0.0 | 0.0 | 0.2 | 0.0 | 122.1 |
| Spain | 21.7 | 12.3 | 7.3 | 28.8 | 8.0 | 5.5 | 10.7 | 0.1 | 3.9 | 1.7 | 0.0 | 253.6 |
| Sweden | 51.4 | 2.4 | 0.1 | 8.2 | 2.2 | 3.8 | 12.2 | 0.0 | 2.2 | 15.6 | 1.9 | 260.3 |
| Tanzania | 10.7 | 10.3 | 9.3 | 18.1 | 11.2 | 12.9 | 7.1 | 7.7 | 3.7 | 3.1 | 5.7 | 248.9 |
| Uganda | 26.8 | 1.8 | 2.1 | 3.2 | 0.3 | 63.6 | 0.9 | 0.4 | 0.1 | 0.4 | 0.4 | 130.3 |
| U.K. | 31.3 | 5.1 | 12.8 | 19.7 | 3.9 | 18.8 | 3.1 | 2.0 | 0.7 | 0.0 | 2.6 | 1120.3 |
| U.S. | 11.8 | 13.4 | 13.6 | 36.7 | 2.7 | 0.0 | 10.2 | 2.2 | 0.9 | 5.5 | 3.0 | 4994.2 |

* Percentages add to 100% across fields.

Source: Johns Hopkins Comparative Nonprofit Sector Project

## Table B.3  Civil society sector FTE workforce, by field, 35 countries

| | Culture | Education | Health | Social Svcs | Environment | Development | Civic / Advocacy | Foundations | International | Professional | Other | Total (thousands) |
|---|---|---|---|---|---|---|---|---|---|---|---|---|
| | Percent* of total civil society workforce | | | | | | | | | | | |
| Argentina | 13.8 | 31.5 | 9.8 | 13.5 | 1.6 | 15.7 | 1.8 | 0.1 | 0.8 | 8.2 | 3.2 | 659.4 |
| Australia | 22.7 | 17.9 | 14.9 | 23.6 | 1.4 | 10.4 | 2.9 | 0.2 | 0.4 | 3.3 | 2.4 | 579.7 |
| Austria | | | | | | n / a | | | | | | 184.3 |
| Belgium | 11.1 | 30.5 | 23.9 | 22.9 | 0.5 | 8.3 | 0.5 | 0.3 | 0.4 | 1.5 | 0.0 | 456.9 |
| Brazil | 15.1 | 35.1 | 17.5 | 19.2 | 0.2 | 3.0 | 0.7 | 0.0 | 0.4 | 8.6 | 0.3 | 1173.8 |
| Colombia | 7.5 | 20.2 | 15.3 | 18.7 | 0.8 | 18.5 | 1.6 | 1.5 | 0.1 | 14.9 | 0.9 | 377.6 |
| Czech Rep. | 35.8 | 10.6 | 11.9 | 13.1 | 6.1 | 6.7 | 3.5 | 2.2 | 1.4 | 8.6 | 0.0 | 115.1 |
| Egypt | | | | | | n / a | | | | | | 629.2 |
| Finland | 32.6 | 12.4 | 13.1 | 15.5 | 0.7 | 1.6 | 16.8 | 0.2 | 0.4 | 6.2 | 0.4 | 137.6 |
| France | 30.0 | 14.6 | 9.2 | 27.4 | 5.0 | 4.7 | 1.9 | 0.6 | 2.4 | 4.3 | 0.0 | 1981.5 |
| Germany | 19.7 | 7.6 | 21.8 | 27.2 | 2.8 | 4.4 | 3.3 | 1.0 | 1.6 | 4.2 | 6.4 | 2418.9 |
| Hungary | 36.8 | 8.9 | 4.7 | 15.1 | 2.2 | 11.3 | 2.3 | 3.7 | 1.0 | 14.0 | 0.0 | 54.8 |
| Ireland | 10.5 | 43.0 | 23.3 | 13.0 | 0.9 | 5.7 | 0.5 | 0.7 | 0.4 | 1.7 | 0.3 | 150.3 |
| Israel | 8.6 | 41.4 | 27.2 | 16.0 | 0.6 | 0.8 | 2.0 | 1.6 | 0.1 | 1.6 | 0.0 | 176.7 |
| Italy | 23.9 | 14.8 | 18.0 | 26.1 | 1.2 | 3.6 | 3.0 | 0.8 | 0.6 | 6.7 | 1.2 | 950.1 |
| Japan | 5.5 | 18.5 | 37.3 | 17.3 | 0.7 | 1.9 | 0.5 | 1.1 | 1.6 | 5.0 | 10.7 | 2835.2 |
| Kenya | 4.7 | 10.8 | 10.1 | 18.6 | 4.0 | 20.2 | 5.3 | 0.3 | 0.0 | 1.5 | 24.5 | 287.3 |
| Mexico | 6.4 | 30.7 | 8.4 | 16.3 | 1.8 | 1.2 | 0.8 | 0.8 | 0.0 | 33.6 | 0.0 | 141.0 |
| Morocco | | | | | | n / a | | | | | | 157.9 |
| Netherlands | 17.2 | 23.1 | 29.5 | 20.3 | 2.0 | 1.7 | 2.9 | 0.2 | 1.2 | 1.8 | 0.0 | 1051.8 |
| Norway | 41.2 | 11.2 | 6.0 | 14.0 | 0.6 | 4.3 | 6.3 | 0.2 | 2.9 | 13.1 | 0.3 | 163.0 |
| Pakistan | 5.2 | 56.6 | 10.4 | 8.0 | 0.3 | 7.8 | 10.0 | 0.0 | 0.0 | 1.7 | 0.0 | 442.7 |
| Peru | 2.5 | 45.2 | 2.6 | 38.3 | 0.4 | 8.8 | 0.5 | 0.9 | 0.0 | 0.9 | 0.0 | 210.0 |
| Philippines | 5.6 | 30.5 | 2.0 | 6.2 | 2.1 | 21.3 | 1.7 | 1.0 | 0.4 | 29.3 | 0.0 | 517.6 |
| Poland | 32.7 | 22.2 | 6.7 | 19.5 | 1.7 | 1.0 | 1.0 | 0.4 | 1.0 | 10.8 | 3.0 | 154.6 |
| Romania | 28.6 | 15.1 | 8.5 | 32.2 | 2.2 | 2.4 | 3.8 | 1.0 | 4.0 | 2.4 | 0.0 | 83.9 |
| Slovakia | 37.0 | 20.4 | 1.9 | 10.1 | 9.0 | 1.1 | 3.8 | 5.6 | 0.9 | 9.1 | 1.1 | 23.0 |
| South Africa | 17.6 | 5.5 | 10.0 | 25.6 | 5.9 | 17.9 | 15.9 | 0.4 | 0.0 | 1.1 | 0.0 | 562.4 |
| South Korea | 4.9 | 40.5 | 25.8 | 15.5 | 0.0 | 0.0 | 9.9 | 0.0 | 0.0 | 3.4 | 0.0 | 535.4 |
| Spain | 15.2 | 20.6 | 10.5 | 30.8 | 3.0 | 9.2 | 5.9 | 0.1 | 2.6 | 1.8 | 0.2 | 728.8 |
| Sweden | 45.5 | 6.8 | 0.9 | 10.5 | 2.1 | 4.4 | 10.2 | 0.2 | 2.3 | 15.4 | 1.7 | 342.9 |
| Tanzania | 10.3 | 11.7 | 10.5 | 16.4 | 10.6 | 12.8 | 7.1 | 7.8 | 3.9 | 3.2 | 5.8 | 330.9 |
| Uganda | 17.7 | 5.3 | 12.8 | 11.2 | 0.9 | 44.8 | 1.9 | 1.4 | 3.3 | 0.6 | 0.2 | 232.9 |
| U.K. | 27.5 | 25.4 | 8.0 | 16.0 | 2.4 | 12.5 | 1.8 | 1.3 | 2.4 | 1.5 | 1.2 | 2536.0 |
| U.S. | 9.0 | 18.5 | 34.2 | 22.1 | 1.0 | 4.0 | 4.9 | 1.0 | 0.3 | 3.9 | 1.1 | 13549.1 |

* Percentages add to 100% across fields.

Source: Johns Hopkins Comparative Nonprofit Sector Project

# APPENDIX C

## CNP Local Associates
## Phases II and IIB

**Argentina**
Mario Roitter
Center for the Study of State and Society

**Australia**
Mark Lyons
University of Technology Sydney

**Austria**
Christoph Badelt
Wirtschaftsuniversität Wien

**Belgium**
Jacques Defourny
Universite de Liège

Jozef Pacolet
Higher Institute of Labour Studies
Katholieke Universiteit Leuven

**Brazil**
Leilah Landim
Instituto de Estudos da Religiâo

**Colombia**
Rodrigo Villar
Confederación Colombiana de ONGs

**Czech Republic**
Martin Potůček/Pavol Frič
Charles University
Institute of Sociological Studies

**Egypt**
Amani Kandil
Arab Network for NGOs

**Finland**
Voitto Helander
Abo Academy

**France**
Edith Archambault
Universite de Paris-Sorbonnes

**Germany**
Eckhard Priller
Wissenschaftszentrum Berlin

Annette Zimmer
Westfalische Wilhelms-Universität Münster

**Hungary**
Éva Kuti/István Sebestény
Central Statistical Office

**Ireland**
Joyce O'Connor/Freda Donoghue
National College of Ireland

**Israel**
Benjamin Gidron
Ben Gurion University of the Negev

**Italy**
Paolo Barbetta
Istituto de Ricerca Sociale

**Japan**
Naoto Yamauchi/Masaaki Homma
Osaka School of International Public Policy

**Kenya**
Karuti Kanyinga/Winnie Mitullah
University of Nairobi

**Morocco**
Salama Saidi
RAWABIT

**Mexico**
CEMEFI
Principal Investigator: Gustavo Verduzco
El Colegio de Mexico, A.C.

**The Netherlands**
Paul Dekker/Ary Burger
Social and Cultural Planning Bureau

**Norway**
Hakon Lorentzen
Institutt for Samfunnsforkning

Per Selle
Norwegian Research Centre in
    Organization and Management

**Pakistan**
Hafiz Pasha
Social Policy Development Centre

**Peru**
Felipe Portocarrero/Cynthia Sanborn
Centro de Investigación de la
    Universidad del Pacífico

**The Philippines**
Ledivina Cariño
University of the Philippines

**Poland**
Ewa Les
University of Warsaw

Jan Jakub Wygnański
KLON/JAWOR

**Romania**
Daniel Saulean
Civil Society Development Foundation

**Slovakia**
Helena Woleková
S.P.A.C.E. Foundation

**South Africa**
Mark Swilling/Hanlie Van Dyk
University of Witwatersrand

**South Korea**
Tae-kyu Park / Chang-soon Hwang
Yonsei University

**Spain**
Jose Ignacio Ruiz Olabuénaga
Centro de Investigación y Desarrollo
    - Estadísticas

**Sweden**
Filip Wijkstrom/Tommy Lundstrom
Stockholm School of Economics

**Tanzania**
Andrew Kiondo/Laurean Ndumbaro
University of Dar es Salaam

**Uganda**
Bazaara Nyangabyaki
Centre for Basic Research

**United Kingdom**
Jeremy Kendall/Martin Knapp
London School of Economics and
    Political Science

**United States**
Lester M. Salamon/S. Wojciech
    Sokolowski
Johns Hopkins University

# APPENDIX D

## International Advisory Committee

***Farida Allaghi***
Saudi Arabia
AGFUND

***Manuel Arango***
Mexico
CEMEFI

***David Bonbright***
Aga Khan Foundation

***Mauricio Cabrera Galvis***
Colombia

***John Clark***
United Kingdom
The London School of Economics

***Pavol Demes***
Slovakia
The German Marshall Fund

***Barry Gaberman***
United States
Ford Foundation

***Cornelia Higginson***
United States
American Express Company

***Stanley Katz***
United States
Princeton University

***Kumi Naidoo***
South Africa
CIVICUS

***Miklos Marschall***
Germany
Transparency International

***John Richardson***
Belgium
European Foundation Centre

***S. Bruce Schearer***
United States
The Synergos Institute

# APPENDIX E

## Project Funders Phase II and IIB

Academy of Finland
Aga Khan Foundation
Associazione Casse di Risparmio Italiane
Associazione Ricreativa e Cultuale Italiana
Australian Bureau of Statistics
Australian Research Council
Austrian Science Foundation
Banca di Roma
Banco di Napoli
Bank of Sweden Tercentenary Foundation
Canadian Fund (Slovakia)
Caritas Ambrosiana
Cassa di Risparmio delle Province Lombarde
Cassa di Risparmio di Puglia
Cassa di Risparmio di Torino
Charities Aid Foundation (U.K.)
Civil Society Development Foundation (Czech Republic)
Civil Society Development Foundation (Romania)
Civil Society Development Foundation (Slovakia)
Colombian Center on Philanthropy
Deutsche Bank Foundation (Germany)
FIN (Netherlands)
Fondation de France
Fondazione Giovanni Agnelli
Fondazione San Paulo di Torino
Ford Foundation (U.S.)
FORMEZ
Foundation for an Open Society (Hungary)
Fundacion Antonio Restrepo Barco (Colombia)
Fundacion BBVA (Spain)
Fundacion FES (Colombia)
Humboldt Foundation/Transcoop (Germany)
Industry Commission (Australia)
Institute for Human Sciences (Austria)
Inter-American Development Bank
Inter-American Foundation
Juliana Welzijn Fonds (Netherlands)
Kahanoff Foundation (Canada)
W.K. Kellogg Foundation

King Baudouin Foundation (Belgium)
Körber Foundation (Germany)
Ministry for Public Administration (Sweden)
Ministry of Church and Education (Norway)
Ministry of Culture and Sports (Norway)
Ministry of Education, Culture and Science (Netherlands)
Ministry of Environment (Norway)
Ministry of Family and Children (Norway)
Ministry of Family/World Bank (Venezuela)
Ministry of Foreign Affairs (Norway)
Ministry of Health and Social Affairs (Sweden)
Ministry of Health, Sports and Welfare (Netherlands)
Ministry of Social Affairs and Health (Finland)
C.S. Mott Foundation (U.S.)
National Department of Planning (Colombia)
National Research Fund (Hungary)
Open Society Foundation (Slovakia)
David and Lucile Packard Foundation
Productivity Commission (Australia)
Research Council of Norway
Rockefeller Brothers Fund
Joseph Rowntree Foundation (U.K.)
Sasakawa Peace Foundation (Japan)
Swedish Council for Research in the Humanities and Social Services
Swedish Red Cross
U.S. Information Service
Yad Hadaniv Foundation (Israel)